whatever it takes

true stories of entrepreneurial imagination, intention & impact

whatever it takes: true stories of entrepreneurial imagination, intention & impact

© 2023 m2 storytellers inc

ISBN 978-1-961185-24-1 (hardcover)
ISBN 978-1-961185-26-5 (paperback)
ISBN 978-1-961185-27-2 (digital)

Cover Design: megs thompson (megswrites llc - www.megswrites.com)
Editing & Layout: megs thompson – (megswrites llc - www.megswrites.com)

www.inomniaparatuspublishing.com
hello@inomniaparatuspublishing.com

this book is for the women who have,
in their own way, done whatever it takes,
to thrive, survive & change lives

table of contents

introduction

This book started with an idea. Well, it actually started long before that idea. Things really started a few decades back when 2 little girls were born on opposite sides of the country. They were raised in separate homes, by separate families & wouldn't know that the other existed until nearly 40 years later.

No, these girls were not twins separated at birth, although sometimes they wonder.

These girls just happened to be soul sisters, twin flames & just the right amount of crazy to complement each other without the need for straight jackets or padded rooms.

Both of these little girls grew up to be young women, facing their own unique obstacles, challenges, heartaches, close calls, highs & lows. And, while there were many times that these 2 young women were a breath away from giving up, giving in, they didn't.

They couldn't.

They knew they were meant for something more.

These 2 young women went to school, got jobs, careers & followed the paths they were told were 'normal.' But they both knew in their hearts that their path wasn't one that was easily found or traveled by others. Their paths were hidden within forests, along mountain ridges, beneath bridges & through swamps.

These 2 young women got married, created families of their own & threw 'normal' out the window.

They birthed businesses, developed brands & found themselves as successful lady bosses in a world filled with far too many 'Karens' & not nearly enough 'Megs' & 'Mandys.'

These 2 young women (alright, fine, they're middle-aged now) finally met one day through the power of the inter-webs & after many coffee dates, Zoom chats & bouts of inappropriate laughter, they conspired to create something.

Something that would encourage other women to share their own uniquely powerful stories with the world. To inspire others with their experiences & accomplishments. To start a ripple of goodness that might go on to touch countless amazing women around the world. To proclaim from the mountain tops (and bookshelves) that they've stumbled, fallen, and done whatever it takes, to get back up; braver, stronger, and more determined than ever before to make their lives their own.

Our mission is to coach, support, empower & encourage women from every walk of life to see their unique lived experiences & stories as having value. Providing them with a safe space to revisit, readdress & rewrite their stories in order to heal themselves & others.

Thank you, to the powerhouse women who trusted us to help bring their stories and experiences to the world.

You are pearls.

Made from grit & full of grace.

Strong, beautiful, powerful & unstoppable.

megs

m² storytellers inc

whatever it takes

stronger
Anita Arredondo

As I sit here, and think back on where I have come from, and where I am now, my heart aches a little, but I also smile, knowing how much I've accomplished so far in my life. It wasn't always easy but it sure was worth it. My name is Anita Arredondo. I am a wife and daughter, a mother, a grandmother, a friend, an entrepreneur, a domestic abuse survivor, a melanoma survivor, and a breast cancer survivor. I was born Anita Cheryl Garcia to my parents, Aida Camero and Augustine Garcia. I have two brothers who are twins, and when my mother woke up after giving birth to me, she couldn't believe it. She finally got her little girl. Growing up my childhood was great, although as I reflect on it now, that was when the emotional abuse started.

I have a clear memory of the night my dad left us. Of a girl standing in the hallway wearing red lace underwear. There was a lot of shouting, a lot of screaming, and I could hear the screeching tires of a station wagon as it left our driveway. That night started the rollout of their divorce, and my mom's custody battle for us kids. I was only three years old at the time, and during the back-and-forth between my dad and mom, I remember not wanting to have to visit or stay with my dad. My biological father was a free spirit. He loved the water and at times it felt as if he preferred his freedom over the responsibility of us kids.

Mom met my stepdad when I was three or four years old and it's a day that I remember vividly. Before they passed away, we used to laugh and joke about that day often. We'd been shopping in Eckerd's, a drugstore much like CVS, and mom was buying us kids candy treats. She saw my stepdad standing across from the store and recognized him as a friend of a friend. Apparently, he'd been trying to hook up with Mom, but she wasn't taking the hint, so, when he saw that I was complaining about the candy she'd picked out for me, he decided to buy me something else. Partly to shut me up, and partly so he could get mom's number and take her out on a date. Their love story was the relationship that I've wanted to emulate ever since, hoping to find my own Prince Charming just like my mom.

They married and because my new stepfather already had four kids of his own, we became a big, blended family, and a real motley crew. We were a Spanish and Italian family that got together for birthdays, events, and holidays. My best memories are of us all together just laughing and loving each other. My stepfather did everything he could to give us the best life possible. And he did just that. My mom was my rock, my best friend, my everything, but my stepfather and I had a special bond that transcended. There were evenings when he would come home from dinner work meetings, sneaking into the house after everyone else was already asleep, with a box of Krispy Kreme donuts under his arm. He'd wake me up and we would sit and enjoy fresh donuts and milk late into the night, talking about life and sharing funny jokes and secrets. He nicknamed me Anitabug, and I was just his little bug. He used to always say, "Go get 'em bug," and I was determined to do just that. He treated my mom like she was his everything and made me feel that was as well.

After they got married, my mom and stepfather purchased a beach house from my grandparents. Every summer after that, we would pack our bags and stay at the beach, only going back home about 3 days before school started again in the fall. Dad worked for the post office, so he drove back and forth to work every day, but mom was a teacher, so she was able to spend the whole summer with us kids at the beach. In true form, mom would make us get a job for the summer, teaching us responsibility, and the value of money. I remember delivering the local paper, it was called the Beach Views Newspaper. Mom would drive the station wagon and I would throw the newspapers out the window. She was always involved in everything that I did. Teaching me lessons that would make me into a better human. We spent our evenings watching beautiful sunsets and walking on the beach. Summers with my mom were a special time. The beach house on Clearwater Beach was a focal point, a gathering place, for everyone to come and spend the day. I remember so many of our family friends coming and having a big giant day at the beach together. My mom would make a big pot of Crab Chilau, and we would spend the entire day as a community with our closest friends. There was so much love that they became like our family. Mom was still close with her friends from high school, and we considered them as aunts and uncles.

When I was young, I wasn't a skinny kid. I had a little bit of a weight problem, and my brothers taunted me about it. They would hold me down and make me do sit ups just to eat a banana. They would make fun of me when they got to eat ice cream and I didn't. They were tall and thin, and I got the genes that made me short and chubby. So, I always had that in the back of my mind, that I was fat, it's something I took that with me into adulthood. I never had a great relationship with my brothers. They were twins so they had each other and didn't need me. Something they made very clear. All I ever wanted was a close sibling relationship, but that wasn't in the cards for me. My brothers may not have needed me, but I had my mom. She was my best friend, my lifeline, my everything.

When I was four, and starting preschool, it was decided to test my IQ. The results came back that I was gifted, and mom was given the choice of leaving me where I was or allowing me to advance to kindergarten right away. This meant I was always a year ahead of the other kids my age, allowing me to graduate high school at 17, and enroll at USF before I turned 18. I lived in the dorm during summer and found friends that had fake id's, went out, partied, and drank. I didn't do well that first summer and when classes started in the fall, things were already going downhill. I think I had a lot of growing up to do but when you are raised by a master's level teacher you don't take a gap year to figure out what you want to do, you just put your head down and do what you're told to. That's what my brothers did. After they graduated from high school, they went off to University of Florida together. I came home from USF when it got to be too much for me, and I moved back in with my mom and stepfather. I got a job and was taking classes at the community college but didn't know what I wanted to do in the future. Because I didn't follow the same path as my brothers, things weren't easy. My decision to not continue my education at USF caused a lot of pain and fighting between mom and me. She was an amazing mother, but she was also very controlling in the fact that she knew what was best for me and didn't understand why I would buck the system.

I remember working at Walgreens at the Westshore Mall back in the 80's. A man walked in who was 2nd cousins with my stepfather. We talked for a few minutes and exchanged numbers. He called me a week later and after we figured out that we weren't actually related by blood, he asked me out. We went on a date and while he was 7 years older than me, I was enthralled with him, his independence, and his desire to take me places. I was 18, he was 25, and I fell hard. Looking back, I don't know if I fell for him because I wanted so badly to get out of the situations I was in at home, or if he was really that great of a guy. While we were dating, I figured out what I really wanted to do in life. I wanted to go to school to be a nurse; I wanted to help others. Pretty quickly, he decided that he wanted to get married. I told him that I wanted to go to nursing school first, and that we could explore getting married a little later. Afterall, I was still so young. He told me that he was ready to get married right then, and that he would not wait. He told me that I could do anything that I wanted to do. I could go to nursing school. He told me that he would support me in that decision. I believed him, so at the age of 20, we decided to get married.

The night of my bachelorette party came, and while my friends spent the evening dancing and having a good time. I spent that time talking and connecting with the man who was driving our limo. To this day I don't remember his name, or what it was about him, but he made a huge impact on me, to the point where we made plans to meet up again the following day. I was so drawn to this man that I'd just met that I knew there was no way I should be getting married. I went to my parents and expressed my concerns, as well as telling my fiancé how I felt. My parents responded by telling me that they had already spent a lot of money on my wedding, and it would not be called off.

The wedding was huge, with 700 people attending, and far too much money being spent. I remember our rehearsal, the night before, at the church. My soon-to-be husband and I were arguing so badly that I tossed his keys at him and went home with my parents in their car. The next morning, I did as I was told, and we were soon husband and wife. I cared about my husband, and at one time I had fallen in love with him, but things had changed. Once we were married, I knew that I wanted a baby. Maybe because I was craving a little best friend, like the connection I'd had with my own mother. We had serious issues getting pregnant. I had to be on fertility pills, which caused my ovaries to grow to the size of grapefruits. I was in and out of the hospital, and finally became pregnant! When we found out it was a girl, it was the best day of my life. I was going to get my little best friend and replicate the special bond my mom and I had. While pregnant, I contracted Hyperemesis, the inability to keep food down, so I had to be on IVs for weeks to get nutrition. As difficult as it was, I was able to make it to 39 weeks.

I remember the day I went into labor. My husband refused to meet me at the hospital. He wanted to go home first to take a shower, get dressed, and get himself situated before we went. He had to look the part of the happy supportive husband and dad-to-be, because that's what he always did, looked the part. He had to make people think that he was something he wasn't. We arrived at the hospital and luckily my mom was there to stay with me. He was hungry, and wanted to go get something to eat at a restaurant while I was in active labor, so he did just that. He got back to my room just in time for me to give birth to our daughter. I was livid and couldn't believe that he thought it was okay to leave me, his wife. But I didn't let that get to me because I had my little girl, I had my little best friend. I had the baby that I longed for; maybe the baby that I needed. The baby that might save me.

We were living in a condominium at the time, but I wanted to build a house of our own. My husband disagreed, but I decided to do it anyway. I drove out to North Tampa and put money down for a lot on the lake to build what would be my dream house. He wasn't very happy about it, but eventually the idea grew on him. We built our house, had an adorable two-year-old whose smile lit up the room, but I knew that I wanted more. I wanted to get an education. I still wanted to pursue my nursing degree, but I quickly learned that the promises he'd made before we got married were empty. I had to pivot and do it quickly. I enrolled in college. I knew I could not be a nurse but I wanted to further my education so I could provide for myself and my daughter. I guess I knew in the back of my mind that this marriage was not going to last forever. It was then that the controlling behavior and emotional abuse started. The daily comments started. *"You're fat. You're ugly. If you're not married to me, you'll never be anything in life." "You can go to school and try to make yourself smart, but you're still not gonna be as smart as me."* The worst was when we would go out together and he would tell people, *"Oh look at little Anita. Didn't I raise her good?"* It was creepy and demeaning. In his eyes the worst thing I could've done was to try and better myself. After working full time, I would pick up the baby at my grandmother's house, then take her home and wait for my husband to get home from the gym so I could race to get to school on time. I had to study in the car because I wasn't allowed to bring my books in the house. When I did get back home there would be dishes in the sink, and laundry piled up waiting for me as punishment. All because I wanted to better myself, educate myself, and do something in life.

During that first year of college, I started losing weight and feeling better about myself. I actually started to feel pretty, despite what my husband told me about how I looked. I found myself connecting with one of my professors, a man who was kind, smart, and said all the right things. He told me that I was smart, I was pretty, I had a lot going for me, and that made all the difference in the world. I remember vividly one day while I was at a friend's baby shower, I wanted to go and be with the person that thought I was all that and a bag of chips. So, I went to my former professor's apartment. He was no longer my professor at the time, and we shared a glass of wine. We talked for hours, and he made me feel like I was the only person in the room. I didn't want that feeling to end, and as I was driving home to my husband and daughter, I knew that our marriage was over. I had already told my husband multiple times that I didn't want to be married to him anymore. He didn't believe me though. When I got home, I had to face the music, telling him honestly where I was, and who I'd been with. I left the house and went to see my brother and sister-in-law who lived around the corner. I knew that she would help shield and care for me.

The divorce proceedings started, but right away, my husband wanted to go to counseling. I agreed to try counseling, but walked in and out the same day because I knew that I wasn't going to continue to live in a marriage or raise my daughter in a home filled with emotional abuse and a lack of support. I moved forward with the divorce, and he proceeded to make that the ugliest time of my life. I moved upstairs because my attorney suggested that I not leave the house, even though my husband was making it nearly impossible for me to exist in the same home as him. But, wanted to be there with my daughter. That all changed one night when he came home from a social club meeting and put his hands on me. I knew at that moment that I was done and needed to get out of there. I called my mother, and she contacted my brother who lived around the corner, and he reluctantly came over to help me leave the house safely. When my brother got to the house, I took my daughter under one arm and a laundry basket filled with clothes under the other, and we left. I went to the place I felt safest, my mom's house.

The next few months felt like a nightmare. Attorneys, depositions, my soon-to-be-ex-husband telling the judge that I tried to stick a coat hanger up my crotch because I wanted to kill my baby when I was pregnant. He said such unimaginable things, and his family was no better, banding together against my family and myself. In the hallway of the courthouse, one of his family members pushed my mother against the wall. There was nothing amicable about the divorce, something his family made sure of. I was so happy when I got an apartment of my own! I was on my way to freedom and independence. I had to go get my belongings out of our house, and while he couldn't be there, neither could my mom, but he made sure that his brother was there, following me around from room to room. Calling me names and treating me like a piece of garbage. I held strong and kept telling myself that this was just temporary, and I would be free soon enough! I had an apartment. I had a job. I had my daughter, And I was happy to be starting a new life. One that was unknown to me but exciting, nonetheless. I remember coming home to my new apartment and having nasty messages on my answering machine from his family members. At times it felt like the emotional abuse would never end. He finally settled on a custody situation, where he was able to see our daughter for one day a week and every other weekend, paying a whopping

$69 a week in child support. He made sure he did everything he could to show that he wasn't making money, and that he couldn't provide anything more for our daughter's needs. I probably wouldn't have made it had I not had the help of my parents, but I was excited about the new journey that I was getting ready to take. I stayed in school, and I continued forward on my path of self-discovery.

During my college years, I'd found a true friend, a best friend, who provided unwavering support and encouragement. Our bond deepened as we navigated life's challenges together, serving as each other's rocks during trying times. This period of self-discovery allowed me to confront my past, rebuild my self-esteem, and find even more strength. Leaving that abusive marriage was a courageous step that marked a turning point in my life, and without her support, I may not have had the courage to take that step.

For the next seven or eight years, I remained single, dedicating myself to my own personal growth and building a strong foundation for my daughter and myself. But then, when I felt like I was ready to explore a relationship for myself again, I was blessed to connect with my soulmate through a dating site. Our connection was immediate and deep, and our love grew rapidly. During our dating process my mother and lifeline contracted cancer. It was not a good prognosis. This new man in my life, my soul mate, was supportive and loving during this process and put together a plan with my parents to propose on the beach near our family house. It was a magical moment. We walked on the sand dune to the very top and I looked over to see my mom sitting outside our beach house watching us. I knew that something special was about to happen. He dropped down to one knee and asked me to spend the rest of my life with him. There was no hesitation, I said, YES! We planned the wedding and moved quickly as my mother needed to be treated for her cancer in another state. We wanted our parents to be there so this was an easy decision for us both. We gave up the wedding we wanted and made it a small, intimate affair, something we put together in only three weeks. My husband-to-be had never been married and this was a truly selfless act on his part. He did all of this for me and my family. His love for me is the truest form of love I've ever felt. The day after the wedding my mother flew out to Houston for treatment and would stay there for the next year or so.

During this time, we enjoyed married life and tried to become a bigger family. Sadly, that was not in the cards for us. We endured 2 miscarriages and did not see any light at the end of the tunnel. But then one day, that light came, and shined brighter than we could ever have imagined. We became a bigger family with our rainbow baby. I didn't think my heart could love another baby like I'd loved my first, but there is something to be said about the love for your first and the love for your last. My heart burst with love for her. Now I had 2 best friends, and my husband was a 100% Girl Dad all the way. My husband was not only a loving partner but also a dedicated father to our child, as well as an amazing stepfather to my eldest daughter. Together, we navigated the complexities of parenthood, facing the challenges and joys it brought. My husband has always said that his job was to raise his daughter like a princess so she would have those expectations when she met the love of her life, and not to accept anything less. He exceeded my expectations as a father and a husband. He is truly my prince charming.

On July 4, 2007, at the age of 60, I lost my mother. She was my heart, my lifeline and a shining light. My life was forever changed. She would always tell me to "be the better person" and I try to make her proud every day. My mother was not just a parent but a source of unwavering support and wisdom, and a true guiding light in my life. My grandmother also stepped up and was an amazing source of love and support until her passing at age 100 in 2021. She would always say "don't let things bother you, just throw it over your shoulder like salt." I'm beyond blessed to have had both of these strong and resilient women in my life to raise me. My mother always said that she would show me a sign that she would always be with me. She did just that. A few weeks after she passed, I was in the pool with my youngest, talking about my mom. I had promised her that I would never let the children forget her, and out of the blue I was swarmed by dragonflies. They hovered and I was immediately brought to tears. It was her; I just knew it. Over the years since her death, dragonflies continue to show up unexpectedly and I know it's my mom, showing me she's still here.

In 2011, during a routine mammogram life presented me with a profound challenge—a diagnosis of breast cancer. This came about a year after a melanoma diagnosis. It was devastating. I remember the day vividly. I was in Publix, my cart filled with groceries, about to check out, when I received the call. They asked me to come in. That is never a good sign. Being the hard head that I am, I insisted on getting answers over the phone. They would not go into detail, only to say that it was not good, and they needed to see me right away. I had a weird feeling of numbness come over me. I called my husband and told him. He told me to leave the groceries, come home, and we would go in together. I insisted that I finish my shopping and check out. Then, only after I'd gotten home and we'd put the groceries away, would we go.

So, we did just that. We held hands tightly when we were told "it is cancer." We were both in shock. This was my first mammogram in my whole life. How could this be? We were immediately scheduled for a biopsy and the process started. After the biopsy we met with the Oncologist. It was Stage 2 Lobular Invasive Carcinoma. It was decision time. The best course of treatment was a Double Mastectomy and Chemotherapy. It was devastating. I remember getting home after all the news and I just sat there quietly, feeling completely overwhelmed with emotion, tears streaming down my face. My husband looked at me and held my hands and said "I am going to give you 2 minutes to have a pity party. You can scream, cry, hit things, whatever you need to do and then when the 2 minutes are up-you need to pull up your big girl panties and be the bad ass woman I married-Now GO!" I cried, screamed, and fell into his arms. It was the most horrible and beautiful experience. Instead of succumbing to despair, I chose to fight with my husband by my side. The battle was grueling. The Chemotherapy was hard, the reconstructive surgeries were painful. But I did it and I am a cancer survivor. I emerged as a survivor with a powerful message and story to tell. My journey led me to become a part of The Affirmations Project. I embraced my body, and had it painted with the affirmation word "Stronger" across my chest bearing my scars as a powerful message that they do not define my beauty or worth. This transformative experience allowed me to inspire others to embrace their bodies, promote self-love, and redefine beauty.

Throughout my breast cancer journey there were days when I felt lost, hopeless, and weak. On most of these days, in true form, I would see signs. Dragonflies would appear, hovering over me and reminding me that my mom was making sure I knew she was up there rooting for me like she always did. It was always a surreal experience, one that made me laugh because I knew exactly what she was doing, but also cry, because of how much I needed her to be here with me. I had made it through and felt stronger and more empowered than ever.

I knew there was more in store for me and that my journey needed to have a purpose. So, in 2020, I founded *Be Healthy Weight Loss and Wellness*, a business dedicated to helping others on their journeys to better health. My approach emphasizes that health is not just about the number on the scale but about nutrition, movement, and, above all, a healthy mindset. Through *Be Healthy*, I have been able to touch countless lives. My clients have experienced remarkable transformations, shedding not only pounds but also the heavy burdens of self-doubt and negative self-perception. Through my own journey to wellness, I am showing others that a healthier and happier life is attainable.

Today, I am blessed with the unwavering support of my husband, a man who sees my inner beauty and intelligence. His love and encouragement have been the driving force behind my transformation. Our love story is a testament to the beauty of finding a soulmate who recognizes and nurtures your inner strength. One who lifts you up and carries you when you need him too. A true soul mate. He remains my biggest supporter, pushing me to excel each day. My life is a testament to the human spirit's resilience. It's a story of turning adversity into opportunity, of healing from the wounds of the past, and of discovering one's true worth. I refuse to let circumstances define me and instead I choose to inspire others to rise above their challenges. The lessons I have learned throughout my life are not just personal triumphs but also invaluable teachings I want to impart to others. I will continue my journey with a deep sense of purpose and a commitment to making a difference in the lives of others. Especially my two daughters.

about the author
Anita Arredondo

Anita Arredondo is the Founder and CEO of Be Healthy Weight Loss and Wellness in Tampa, Florida. She has a bachelor's degree in business and an associate degree in marketing, plus a Certification in Nutrition Coaching. Her passion is helping others change their mindset about food and learn to live and no longer diet. Whether her clients are struggling with self-image, weight issues, or just need nutritional guidance, she meets clients where they are and works with them to recognize and overcome self-sabotaging behaviors; helping create new, positive habits. She truly wants others to get healthy and Be Healthy. Born and raised in Tampa, Florida, she is a former single mother and now a devoted wife of 21 years to Tony and a loving mother to her daughters Ashleigh (31) and Alyssa (19). She takes immense joy in being a grandmother to Anthony and Amelia.

Anita's passion lies in music and concerts, and she cherishes spending time with friends. Anita's resilience shines through as a survivor of both Melanoma and Breast Cancer, as well as a survivor of domestic abuse from her ex-husband. She once graced the stage as a dancer during the

Super Bowl halftime show in Tampa in 1984. She is involved in The Affirmations Project where in 2016 she had her body painted with the word "Stronger" across her chest after a double mastectomy and reconstruction, to provide hope to others that there is life after cancer, to promote self-love, and show that our scars do not define us. Notably, she's also a published author, known for her work in "*Slaying Tampa Bay*." Her life philosophy is beautifully summarized in her belief that in life, every obstacle she encounters is not a roadblock, but a steppingstone to making her "Stronger." You can find her at www.behealthytampa.com or under Anita Garcia Arredondo on Facebook and Anitabug0305 on Instagram.

healing is a choice
Jennifer Day

E ach of us has a story based on our own personal truths and perspectives of our lives. What makes us feel love, joy, surprise, sadness, anger, and fear? Do you know how those emotions show up in your body, your life, and what they are meant to tell you? For the longest time, I didn't. Heck, sometimes I still don't – but I'm here and I'm prioritizing myself, my healing, my life, and my happiness, a little bit more each day.

We are all works in progress, no one is perfect, but this snippet is a glimpse into my experience of working through the voices of others that held residence in my head for far too long. This is my story of doing whatever it takes to work through the lowest parts of my life, and in doing so, emerging as the woman I am today. A woman filled with passion, courage, curiosity, hope, and peace. Writing and sharing this part of my story has allowed me to revisit and reconcile with some very heavy negative emotions and feelings. Numbness, judgment, shame, guilt, grief, rejection, and fear.

I chose to participate in this book project so that others might feel seen, heard, valued, and acknowledged too. Life can be messy. Healing is a choice that can be painful, often described as not being for the faint of heart; however, choosing to heal already means that you are strong!

Growing up there was always something in the back of my mind that made me feel like I wasn't supposed to be seen, heard, or acknowledged. It filled me with feelings of being unworthy and unlovable, and one of my childhood survival tactics became being able to read the behaviors of others, matching my behaviors to what was needed to keep me emotionally safe. All so that I might stay loved and not feel abandoned.

As a child of the 70s, most of the neighborhood kids played outside until they were called in for dinner. I spent much of my time inside, in front of the TV. Mom was the epitome of the "white glove cleaning lady." She was a stay-at-home mom and at the time it seemed like her sense of purpose was to raise us kids through her cooking and housework before she would need to go back to work outside of the home when I was in my late teens. Honestly, I don't feel like I remember her enjoying any of that time. It seemed like she followed the societal norm of what was expected of her, whether that was her truth or not, and did not make herself a priority, setting aside time or space for friends or hobbies. I grew up knowing that I did not want that for my own life.

As a result, I never really felt emotionally connected to Mom as a child. She was, however, a very emotional woman. Her sadness, excitement, frustration, and anger all came out in the form of tears. I am certain that she was depressed much of her life. And, while depression was common on her side of the family, she would never acknowledge it. Instead, choosing to suffer through the sadness.

I am a combination of my mom and dad, learning how to communicate, feel, and process emotions from them both. As happens with each new generation, they mirrored or changed what they had learned from their own parents while raising me. I learned early on that my authority figures also had struggles of their own, and that having big emotions as a child was not welcome. I always felt like they were supposed to be pushed down as my needs could not be met. We've all heard it before, a parent telling their child not to cry when they've fallen and scraped their knee.

How does this relate to weight and self-worth? Well, from an early age, food became a comfort. I would either blatantly want more or would sneak food into my closet to eat in secret (aka binge eating). I was a kid after all, and I had no idea what a kid size portion was or how that related to my overall health. My cravings were always for sweets, and I was certain that somehow a candy bar or bigger piece of cake would soothe the uncertain feelings I was experiencing. My brain registered the dopamine hit that sugar creates which can mimic effects of addiction and increase cravings and sugar tolerance.

At one point in my life, when I reached my highest weight of 325 pounds, I avoided full length mirrors altogether. How did I allow myself to do that? I tried all kinds of things to lose weight. As an adult I went to Weight Watchers and Jenny Craig, I tried Nutrisystem, different high protein, low carb diets, hypnosis, starvation, the cabbage soup diet, and was even scheduled for gastric bypass surgery at one point. Thankfully, changes with my insurance coverage led to that surgery being cancelled two weeks before it was set to take place.

Negative self-talk around my weight as a child was just a part of my daily life. I remember being incredibly young and going to Weight Watchers with my mom and Grandma, learning through those meetings that my weight and appearance were my identity, and they became what I based my self-worth on. Many of my childhood memories around my weight were brought on by comments made by family members. Maybe this will resonate with you too?

"You're such a pretty girl ... if you'd only lose some weight."

My Mom was an only child and her father, my grandfather, was an avid hunter and angler. As a child, it always felt like he wanted a grandson, not a granddaughter. He may have even preferred to have a son versus the daughter he had. I never addressed those thoughts with my parents, and I wonder now if my mom ever felt the same. She struggled with her weight most of her life and we were always trying some "diet."

Around age 11 or 12 my maternal grandfather, perhaps to motivate me, had a talk with me about being fat. He informed me that, *"Fat is ugly. Boys do not like fat. And if they do, they're coming from a toad pond and not the ocean."* With all those negative feelings about my body, I became extremely self-conscious, told myself I was not good enough, worthy, or lovable. Seriously, how would you have felt, being made to wear a girdle (currently known as shapewear, although those were much more constricting back then) as a child just to go out in public?

Being of Polish descent, the women on the maternal side of my family were not small, and yet they all found love, got married, had kids, and lived happily ever after. I thought for sure that I could do the same! I never realized how that trauma would influence so many of the decisions I'd make later in my life or how those negative emotions could be stored in my body. The concept of body positivity was around by that point, although not something discussed in my household. If only someone realized that separating my worth from my body image is what I needed most. Now we know this in the current day as *Body Neutrality* and it's become something that I'm extremely passionate about!

In my teens, I cut soda out of my diet and tried to avoid eating sweets as much as possible. Based on my weight, I chose not to try out for the cheerleading squad (although I have a loud, boisterous voice). While I really wanted to, I told myself that they didn't have cheer uniforms in my size anyway. (Any chance that I can get an apology for the curves that I had naturally as a teen, that others pay to have these days? Lol, I digress.) I did make the softball team as a catcher yet struggled to feel confident under the pressure of being good enough to help my team.

There were several relationships in my teens and early twenties with men that were older than myself. I hoped that they would have matured past the judgmental stage of life (not looking at my own judgment) and how my body image affected me. One day in my late teens, I was spending time with a co-worker after we'd cashed out our checks. He wanted me to drive us to his house to give his mom some money. I am certain that he knew she would not be home and he tried to force himself on me. I managed to push him away and flee before anything happened. I didn't understand how a guy that I liked, and that liked me, was going to force me into something I didn't want to do. After that, going to work felt extremely uncomfortable and I had to tell Management and Security what happened. Learning that he had tried the same thing with other girls at work made me feel even worse about myself. It almost validated that I was unlovable and unworthy of something good.

Fast forward and I became a mom at 24. No one could really tell that I was pregnant until the very end. I only gained 13 pounds with my daughter, but because I was already heavyset, I just went up in the size of my usual clothes. In fact, most of my adult life at that point had been bouts of hiding under roomy clothes so that my figure could not be seen. Hoping that I wouldn't be judged.

I continued to question my self-worth through internal and external judgment and would go through bouts of self-loathing and anxiety/depression throughout much of my adult life. I knew that I needed help to understand why I was not losing weight and not feeling good enough, worthy, or lovable. Initially, I tried various therapists for CBT (Cognitive Behavioral Therapy) which only dealt with surface issues and never came close to the deep-rooted unhealed trauma that was the foundation.

In review of my two, six-year, emotionally abusive relationships, before and after my daughter's birth, both created some serious trust issues, poor decisions, and ultimately resulted in two bankruptcies. I learned just how drastically my self-worth and lack of boundaries could affect me. Oh yes, let's add a failed marriage in between those two relationships, after learning that my (ex)spouse was leaving my 2-year-old at home alone while he "ran errands." During our divorce, it became clear that those "errands" had a name. Talk about throwing any form of self-care out the window, which included my eating! I got myself into an EAP program through work and used the support of family and friends to get through that year plus of stress, rescheduled court dates, and weeks of chasing the ex from one place to the next as he continuously attempted to avoid paying child support.

During my daughter's teen years, we butted heads like moms and daughters typically do. Without realizing it, I passed on critical thoughts about her body image by making a comment about her tummy in a particular dress she had picked out to wear for a special dance at school. It was not intentional, and I am truly sorry that she had to experience that through her mom. Sadly, she didn't mention the comment or how it affected her until she was an adult and had children of her own.

There were times where I questioned whether I was worth anything, and if I even wanted to be a part of the world anymore. The practical side of me pondered who would watch my daughter and my dogs. The irrational side of me did not care. I just wanted all the pain and hurt to end. I had noticed patterns and was not sure what to do with them. I have been told that you repeat the same lesson over and over until you learn what is needed. I have spent most of my life in survival mode. Fight, flight, freeze, and fawn (people-pleasing) were absolutely on autopilot and second nature to my everyday life. What I learned is that all those behaviors were protecting me in an intelligent way for the times that it needed to, and I was not just being a stubborn ass (every single time)! In not knowing what to do or how to feel my emotions completely, my body would freeze, and I would be unable to make any decisions. You can imagine how that would take a toll on a body. That unhealed past trauma stuff is what traps our emotions in our bodies, creating a "stuck" feeling and keeps us from moving forward later in life. I can remember extremely specific times in my life where I experienced those exceptionally low points and used food as a coping mechanism by either eating everything in sight to stuff down my feelings or deciding to not eat at all, as a form of self-punishment.

2015 was a year that seemed to be filled with those exceptionally low points. The entire year revolved around the two women who played a huge role in my life, and my becoming the woman I am today. My mom and my daughter. My Mom had many health issues and underwent countless surgeries during her adult life. We would have never guessed though that when she went to the hospital on the eve of my daughter's 16th birthday party, she would not come home. Instead, she'd spend 5 ½ months bouncing back and forth between hospitals and rehab centers until she passed away.

During that time, my daughter was struggling with a bullying situation online while recovering from breaking her ankle, which required surgery. During this stressful time, she became focused on hurting herself and misusing her pain medication. I got her some help, but I could not say anything to my parents at the time as they were dealing with my mom's health issues and the potential of her being released from rehab and potentially moving into my home temporarily.

While I was in a typical mom-daughter struggle with my mom for most of my own young life, I was extremely grateful to have had her to watch my daughter for the first 6 months of her life so that as a single parent I did not have to worry about her being in daycare or with strangers immediately. My parents helped me raise her as her own dad and stepdad both opted to be out of the picture.

It was not until I processed that I would no longer be able to ask my mom the important questions I might have, that it hit me. This was permanent. She was gone and wasn't coming back. But I HAD to keep my shit together for my dad and my daughter. Dad needed me more than ever as he and mom had been married for 44 years, and he was lost without her. Mom was a HUGE part of my daughter's life, and losing her grandmother caused a relapse in her ability to access her coping skills. I can still clearly remember the day I got the call that I needed to rush home. Immediately. My daughter was looking to hurt herself. I was riding my Harley, and as I rounded the corner onto our block, I could see my daughter on the ground, surrounded by paramedics and state police. My heart sank not knowing what had happened. Dear God, I could not lose her too! After overnight observation, she came home, and I learned to be hypervigilant over any potential signs of her hurting herself again. During this time, my focus was on my family and trying to process the grief. I was not using my coping skills to the best of my ability. I was numbing my feelings with food, lack of food, or alcohol. In fact, recently I worked through another layer of that grief, not realizing that it was still here.

In 2016, after a family trip, the decision was made to begin the process of relocating once my daughter graduated from high school in 2017. The excitement was brewing, and the stress began. By March of 2017, my house was on the market and went under contract within a week. It sold at the end of May, and I coordinated living arrangements with family and friends until my daughter's high school graduation in June. She, her then boyfriend, now husband (aka the kids), my then partner and I took the vehicles, the cat, three dogs and a 26-foot rental truck, and drove for almost 2 full days to our new life. Traveling can be tough on our nervous systems and finding healthy foods while on the road can be a struggle. But we didn't care at the time, our focus was on a fresh start in a new home and a new state.

I purchased my house the day after arriving and it took a bit of time to get settled in. Early stressors with the new house made me panic about money, which then caused a ripple effect of not focusing on fueling my body well. I was devastated when the kids announced their pregnancy and their decision to move back 'home' after less than 5 months of being in our new home. My only baby, who was now having a baby of her own, was moving away, and I was locked into a mortgage here. I used food and alcohol to cope. By no means was it an alcoholic situation; however, I knew that alcoholism had been a factor in other members of my family, so I have always known to be vigilant of my own consumption.

In 2018, things seemed to continue falling apart after only a year in my new home. This time, it was yet another failed relationship. This person had a good heart but was not yet ready to address his own healing, which held him back from showing up in our relationship in the ways I needed. I mirrored back to him what we both needed to heal. After he left, I found myself with an excess of time on my hands and an incredible sense of abandonment. A feeling I'd experienced many times before. There was a loneliness in living in a 1,500 square foot home as a single woman with my three dogs and a cat.

That was not what I had planned for when we had the dream of moving to warm weather, palm trees, pelicans, and dolphins. Who coordinates a home sale, watches a high school graduation, completes a house purchase in another state, and then less than a year later finds herself alone again? Sitting with myself did not feel comfortable at that time. I had to get a handle on my eating at that point. I would weigh myself daily and chose to eat whatever I wanted to. If I did not like the number on the scale, I would barely eat at all. I was struggling to control anything in my life and that was my attempt to regain it.

With all this time on my hands in early 2019, I decided that I need to get out of the house and get busy. So, I enrolled in massage therapy school. I would work full-time Monday through Friday, go to school at night Monday through Thursday, and then work clinics on Saturday mornings. In between, I would go out dancing with friends on Fridays and/or Saturday nights.

This is when I began the journey of wanting to lose weight again. I would do my cooking and homework on Sundays. Sounds like a fantastic way to constructively stay busy and learn a new skill, right? WRONG! Busy was just an effortless way to mask and avoid working through the feelings of abandonment, loneliness, sadness, depression, and anything else that came up.

I met (what I thought was) a charming, funny guy towards the end of 2019 through work. I let things move too quickly. I thought I was in a place where I had my shit together, which made me feel ready to try again at love. All the narcissistic red flags were there, but I didn't see any of them until we were already in the thick of things. He moved in with me in January of 2020, and life seemed great at first. Both of us worked in construction on the same hospital projects. While the rest of the world seemed to have shut down for COVID, these projects were expansions for extra patient beds so there was no break or working from home for us. COVID was a huge stressor for the world. So many people developed terrible eating habits during their downtime while others used their time at home to focus on new, healthier habits. As I focused on being better equipped for healthier eating at work, I made sure to keep healthier snack options in my desk drawer to avoid the kitchen area of donuts, pizza, and various sweet treats on a regular basis. Afterall, these were construction jobsites.

In May, he was in a serious accident on our jobsite, and it took almost an entire year for him to recover. I was stressed out. I threw my focus on healthy eating out the window again and as our relationship changed in a big way, again I used food to cope with the changes. One day while bringing in groceries (because anyone who is a mom knows that we often bring in multiple bags at once to take less trips), I overdid it and hurt my shoulder. For weeks, my collarbone was protruding forward, and the muscles were sore. I tried to ignore it, like many stubborn people do, (my family is full of stubborn people, lol) but in August, the pain began radiating down into my bicep and it was time to have it looked at. Thank goodness that I did!

On October 13, 2020, I was wheeled out of the hospital with a cancer diagnosis. I had no idea WTH a Carcinoid Tumor, aka Neuroendocrine Tumor (NET), was or what was next. I was not sleeping or eating well. I spent every waking moment researching what it was, connecting with support groups, and going to a slew of doctor's appointments which all led to my needing surgery for the larger tumor which was blocking 85-90% of the main airway of my left lower lung lobe.

We are often so busy doing life that we forget to show up for ourselves. Our bodies are wired to tell us when they need something. A friend recently shared that she views trauma and life challenges pertaining to the body as a "feather (first warning), a brick (second warning), or a Mack truck (last warning)." This is where we can find ourselves extremely sick or experiencing muscle aches and pains that are not just part of the aging process. These are the things that show up in DIS-EASE of the body, including IBS, arthritis, diabetes, heart disease, high blood pressure, cancer, etc. These are the warning signs that we too often choose to ignore. *"When The Body Says No (the cost of hidden stress)"* is a fascinating scientific book by Gabor Mate, who speaks on how trauma is stored in the body and how it shows up, regardless of what you are doing in life.

After a bumpy road of having to switch doctors and hospitals, I had my golf ball size NET and left lung lobe removed in February of 2021. The smaller tumor would stay where it was and be monitored over the next 5-10 years. With COVID still happening, no one was allowed to stay overnight at the hospital with me. The only other time that I had been an overnight patient in a hospital was when I had my daughter. I was a scared, stubborn patient, yet determined to do what I was told and get back home as quickly as possible. Although six weeks of recovery was not horrible, I know that I pushed myself because I did not want cancer and my remaining tumor to define me. As I recovered, I felt a sense of having a new lease on life. I wanted to do better for myself and my family. I found a new cardio exercise hobby that I really enjoyed. I started a new job in May and things were looking up. It was easier to focus on eating healthier (even though I did have lobster tails with drawn butter a few times during recovery as a welcome home gift from dad, lol).

In June of 2021, I experienced something that damn near broke me, much like coming home to chaos with my daughter in Sept 2015. This time it made me question everything about who I was and who I thought I was. No one who'd met my partner or I during our 2+ years together saw this shock coming, and it made me feel like I had lost myself. I felt like I could never trust myself again! Many of my closest friends & family were worried about my ability to bounce back.

While I had experienced emotionally abusive relationships in my past, this was different. This was a whole new level of utter manipulation. All I could think of was that my grandfather was right, that my weight was the factor that messed with my self-esteem, and I kept attracting the wrong people. Thinking I would always have to settle for who looked my way, instead of me getting to CHOOSE someone worthy of my time and energy.

I never knew what the signs of a narcissist were before then, and oh shit, did I learn them all the fast and furious way! For two plus years, this person had lied about who he was, sharing with me the most vivid details of things that had NEVER happened. He was the epitome of insecurity, and he genuinely believed every word he spoke! The life that I thought we had together, including our pending marriage, was a complete farce!

I mean, c'mon, I had been working on my physical and mental health over the past few years of healing and thought I was a good judge of character, could spot red flags, and believe what my body was telling me. *"How could I have been so dumb,"* was a question I asked myself constantly for the 3 weeks following his erratic and scary departure. For me, and most everyone, the one place that you get to be yourself, no matter what is going on in the world or inside your body, is your home! I felt violated in a way that I could never describe. I buried myself in 12–14-hour days at work to numb the pain and barely ate anything for the next 3 weeks. I could not force much of anything down. I lived off protein coffee, protein shakes, and the adrenaline of chaos that ensued during that time. My nervous system was beyond jacked up and dysregulated! Trusting myself after a major blow like that hurt much worse than my divorce in the early 2000's ever did.

Like so many times before, that experience would teach me so much about myself. This time it was a slap in the face. A true test of dedication I would need to put in to find myself again. I struggled with grace and compassion. It took me a bit to get back on track, fueling my body with nutrients and focusing on getting stronger.

I was reminded, yet again, that I have persistence, determination, willpower, and hope. If all the previous experiences in my life did not take me out, this would not either. I got myself back into counseling to work through learning how to trust myself again. I realized that while I have done surface work to heal, the habits and patterns remained the same. It had to stop. I was experiencing a level of insanity in so many relationships. I was trying to prove my worth all along. I began to recognize that at some point those friendships or romantic relationships were not serving me.

Why did I want what was best for others but not for myself? I needed answers. It was a sinking feeling like a failure of myself, instead of just failing others. And this was a familiar feeling; however, it was different this time. It became my opportunity to figure out how to never feel this way again.

In mid-May of 2022, I connected with a woman online who is a Trauma-Informed Somatic Coach. Little did I know that joining her 6-month cohort would begin a different level of inner work that opened my eyes to how I showed up in my life. I knew I had things from my childhood that still affected me, but I did not realize to what level. I started discovering boundaries, relationship patterns and really starting to understand what self-love was about.

While going out to run errands by myself was no big deal, taking myself on a date seemed excruciating. Just like I had experienced before, when I walked into a new location for weight loss, the gym, or even a restaurant for dinner, I could feel the judgmental eyes on me. Questioning why I was showing up alone. I used to dread getting on an airplane and having to ask for a seat belt extender. And, as humans do, I created a story around what that meant to others, to those watching and judging me, when in truth, it did not mean a damn thing to anyone else but me. No one was really paying attention and if they were they might have struck up a casual conversation. I very distinctly remember one of the first calls in the cohort, my mentor advised that changes may occur during this process of healing. The surprise of what happened next now helps me feel empowered.

In September, while visiting my family up North, I walked my hometown green with a beautiful energetic friend. She and I had been contemplating ways for me to get health insurance coverage if I moved on from a toxic corporate job and into a massage practice of my own. Before we hugged each other goodbye that morning, my boss was calling me with HR on the line. It turned out that I was one of four on the chopping block from our department as the company had been bought out months prior and departments were being merged. That afternoon, I drove to the local cemetery to sit with my grandparents' headstone, hoping to connect with my mom as well. I sat on the ground, cried, rocked back and forth, and wondered if I had manifested this to happen (the answer was yes). Instant panic set in. How was I going to pay the bills? Why now? I am not ready. Time has a way of helping us figure things out. Once I returned home, I coordinated my next place to move and focused on creating new experiences in life after selling my home. I was so burnt out that I gave myself permission to take the rest of 2022 to heal. It was not until this level of permission that I really began to understand the need to fuel my body and learn that resting was not lazy. I gave myself permission to focus on what I wanted, maybe for the first time in my life! I managed to drop almost thirty pounds in total before the end of 2022 and was feeling so much more like myself again.

Fast forward to my life right now in 2023. I am now a published author, a Certified Energy Therapist, Licensed Massage Therapist, Certified Trauma-Informed Somatic Coach, a Certified DRUMFIT® Cardio Drumming Instructor and have two pending Certifications for ChakraDance Facilitator, and Nutrition Coach in the works. I have been out of a corporate job for over a year now. I have started experiencing so many positive changes in my healing journey which has also brought the start and close of a business location, along with ending many inauthentic friendships. It has also opened my eyes which lead to the start of my second business following my passion of coaching and helping others on their transformative journey towards sustainable weight loss and personal growth. I even participated in a Body Positivity modeling event earlier this year which was inclusive of sizes 0 to 4X. I had to physically experience that I no longer fit in my "normal" size for the event. Talk about being elated!

Until this year, I had never heard of Brene Brown, but in listening to her many videos, TEDx talks, Podcasts, Netflix special and books, she's introduced me to what is known as "The Man in The Arena" speech. It comes from "*Citizenship in a Republic*," a speech given by Theodore Roosevelt, former President of the United States, at the Sorbonne, in Paris, France, on April 23, 1910:

"It is not the critic who counts; not the man who points out how the strong man stumbles, or where the doer of deeds could have done them better. The credit belongs to the man who is actually in the arena, whose face is marred by dust and sweat and blood; who strives valiantly; who errs, who comes short again and again, because there is no effort without error and shortcoming; but who does actually strive to do the deeds; who knows great enthusiasms, the great devotions; who spends himself in a worthy cause; who at the best knows in the end the triumph of high achievement, and who at the worst, if he fails, at least fails while daring greatly, so that his place shall never be with those cold and timid souls who neither know victory nor defeat. Shame on the man of cultivated taste who lets refinement to develop into fastidiousness that unfits him for doing the rough work of a workday world."

He was pointing out that it is easy to criticize others, but it takes real courage to be the person who is in the arena, doing the work and facing challenges head-on. This can be in the workplace, in relationships, personal growth, etc. This is where people expect us to cave in and give up. Thankfully, I have outgrown those types of people and now realize that I get to choose me, fully. Not the voices in my head, not the learned behaviors from my childhood, and certainly not the judgment from others who do not have the courage to be brave and put themselves out there!

Brene Brown has a powerful quote that's stuck with me during this time. *"Vulnerability is not winning or losing; it's having the courage to show up and be seen when we have no control over the outcome. Vulnerability is not weakness; it's our greatest measure of courage."*

Perhaps the purpose of these most recent experiences was more about life realization, getting curious about the experience, feeling it, healing it, and using it as redirection on the highway of life. I have never resonated with the "fake it 'til you make it" concept. At several points in my life, I've felt like I was floundering and truly unsure what moving forward should look like. It was only once I became aware of my patterns and learned some healthy ways to regulate myself, that my thought process began to change. And while this may not resonate with some of you immediately, it will eventually.

The new motto I live by is "feel it to heal it." There are things in life that bring us discomfort and we often run away (flight in our nervous systems) to alleviate that pain. It could be food, drugs, gambling, sex, etc.

Recently in a somatic experience with my mentor, something came up very strongly for me. I immediately tried to kick into action the somatic practice exercises I am certified in and now know how to use. But this time was different. My mentor challenged me to see if my body would allow me to sit with the intensity of the emotion. Although I sat in discomfort for a bit, the part that came next was profound. She gave me cues and props to work through the feeling I was having. In this way, I didn't stop the process part way through but rather "rode the wave" of completion so that I could heal it. She often uses the concept of holding a beach ball under the water, with it immediately springing to the surface. If we can relate that to emotions and sensations in our bodies, it works in the same exact way. We use the various coping mechanisms we have, to stop things or push them down, and yet we wonder why we aren't getting different results each time we try something new.

So, who makes those decisions these days? It's not the child version of Jenn. The one who heard the voices of authority figures and followed without hesitation. It's now the continually healing adult version, Jenn, who is a completely different woman than I was even at the beginning of this year!

I still struggle as I am a Neurodivergent Queen with ADHD, anxiety and former binge eating tendencies; however, I am beyond blessed with some incredible connections made within a group of women entrepreneurs in my life who are not only my mentors but have become friends. In my mind, having them as both is important because this work is so very personal. In fact, my entire tribe, family, and a small group of trusted friends, is made up of those who can relate to me through their own healing journeys in life. I am worthy of showing up for myself and these people not only listen but hold space for my own realizations to arrive when I need them. As I heal, change my perspective and how I show up in my relationships with them, I notice that it gives them permission to show up differently as well.

Over the last year and a half, I have worked with multiple modalities to help clear some of this conditioning from my childhood and adult life. Including those who practice Chakra

Balancing, Reiki, Integrated Energy Therapy, Massage, EMDR, Trauma-Informed Somatic Coaching, Human Design, EFT Tapping, and several mentors who support the mind/body connection.

The growth I've experienced has been beautiful and challenging and scary AF! The difference this time is that I'm honoring myself through all of it. I'm being honest with myself and discovering what makes me "me" probably for the first time in my life. I honestly don't know what's next, and I focus on not feeling constantly pressured to have all the answers right now. My mentor reminds me often that "more will be revealed" when the timing is right, and she is right. The lessons happen at various times and the 'aha' results can come when they're meant to. Besides, if you have it all clearly mapped out, is it really your life that you're living or someone else's?

I am now experiencing the healthiest relationship that I have ever been in. It is scary for both of us. Being vulnerable is not easy. We talk about what is coming up for us a lot. Some days I want to run when discussions get heavy and sometimes, I feel small in anticipation of an unfavorable response. It takes me time to ask if what I am telling myself is true? Do I have evidence of —-- (whatever)? Some days, I feel his angst of needing time to sort through the same. The unique gifts we have and bring to each other are new to both of us. It involves patience, understanding, compassion, connection, honesty, trust, the ability to hold safe space for the bad days, and to celebrate the good days. There is continued growth for both of us. We're learning to speak our truths and ask for what we need. One of the most important gifts for my weight loss journey, that I haven't always had, is how he supports me. I do not have to fight my way through food temptations brought into the house. We are both committed to eating healthier 95% of the time and we do our own types of exercise. I do love that we both have sweet tooths though, so I have plenty of creative low sugar and sugar-free treats as work arounds for us. We even cook together!

With all that being said, my caterpillar to butterfly journey took a lot of time and was EXTRA gooey. That (isolation) time in the cocoon felt like it took forever! It was another representation to me that healing is not linear, and while much of it is done on your own, the rest is done in relationships and friendships with others. We are like onions with multiple layers and what we thought we had healed on layers 5, 7, 19, 36, can come back up at layer 57 as it relates to interaction with others.

Your tribe and those you meet on your path will challenge you to be certain that you are really in it for the long-haul and have learned the lesson(s) necessary. The butterfly in me has just emerged and her wings are still drying. I'm stepping into the most authentic, peaceful life in a healthier body that I now call home. I no longer hate my body, instead I honor the path that it has supported all these years. THIS IS HUGE in my venture to heal generational trauma around weight, judgment, shame, and guilt. Trust the process are not just words you hear. It's a feeling that comes when you're leveling up in growth and awareness. Healing doesn't happen when we want it to and it's important to accept that it doesn't often look how we think it will, once we've embodied what we've learned. In learning to lean into my womanhood and fully being a woman, appreciating the gifts of life – my daughter recently welcomed her second son into the world, without medication during labor. It has shown me that I am a strong woman, who raised a strong woman and I'll take that win!

Let's get back to the weight, weight loss, and how it all connected for me. I needed to discover what the "*Weight of Armor*" was protecting me from? How was it serving me? Why did I need to hold on to it?

I don't have all the answers so I'm not going to BS you. What I do know is that releasing the shame, guilt, and judgment that surrounded what I thought was my identity for my entire life has been life changing. It has required me to be extremely honest and rediscover what makes me tick. It's been a time of learning to take everything off the table of life, starting with a clean slate. My original Mentor and friend reminded me that "we teach what we need to learn." She couldn't have been more correct. The judgment and thoughts we have about ourselves are so often a reflection about what others have said. I'm doing the work and healing the traumas, assumptions, negative thoughts and understanding that my body has been in survival mode and was intelligently protecting me all this time.

I used to live my life questioning why *THIS* was happening to me? Along the way, I've learned that we tend to think we are the only ones in the story that matters. Now it's more like this is happening *FOR* me. I used to chase my self-worth through outside validation in my work and relationships.

I encourage you to look at what's on your plate and ask yourself if you are experiencing the joy and happiness that you want for yourself? Are you over committed? Numb and going through the motions? Using food as a reward or punishment? Still holding on to patterns that you know are no longer serving you? Are you ready to be honest with yourself so that you can also find your peace and create the life you've always dreamed of?

So many life adversities...and yet, I'm still here!

I want to inspire anyone going through similar situations, or a series of bumps in the road of life, to understand that sustainable change(s) can be made to create a happy, joyful, and authentic life for yourself. I get to impact the lives of others through my knowledge and life experience. I've been where you are, and can meet you there, supporting you in achieving your goals. This can include deciding what lights you up or discovering what holds you back in life, resolving past unhealed trauma, or specifically for me, how a number on the scale created my self-worth and what the potential "Weight of Armor" is doing for you by separating your emotions from your body. This is called Body Neutrality, literally saying that you have a body that needs to be fueled and moved. No focus on tall, short, fat, or thin. We can work on how to heal what is holding you back and watch the transformation of viewing your body as a vessel to get you there with compassion and grace.

Whether you decide now is the time or not yet, know that you are not alone. There is a village of people who come to help us during our healing and I'm happy to walk your journey with you!

I cannot stress this enough, the most important relationship you'll ever have in this lifetime is the one with yourself. "*I am enough. I am worthy. I am loveable. I am powerful. I am multi-passionate.*" I now fully see and choose me. You can choose this too!

whatever it takes

about the author
Jennifer Day

Jenn is a multi-passionate entrepreneur who specializes in assisting clients on their transformative journey towards sustainable weight loss and personal growth. Her multifaceted expertise encompasses certifications in trauma-informed somatic coaching, integrated energy therapy, massage therapy, DrumFIT® cardio drumming coaching, ChakraDance® facilitation, and nutrition coaching with a focus on Body Neutrality techniques and somatic movement.

Her entrepreneurial spirit was ignited after she overcame personal challenges, including a corporate burnout, Neuroendocrine cancer surgery, and the management of neurodivergent conditions such as anxiety, depression, ADHD, and binge eating tendencies. Through her personal struggles with weight loss, she realized the importance of addressing

underlying issues, including childhood trauma, to achieve lasting success. After 27 years of experience in the construction industry, Jenn's administrative and project management skills have seamlessly transitioned into her entrepreneurial career, where she empowers others to achieve their goals. She approaches every aspect of her work with expertise, authenticity, and unwavering integrity.

She lives in the Tampa Bay Area of Florida with her two rescued fur babies. She loves multiple forms of travel and goes to see her family (including two grandsons) & friends in the Northeast as often as she can. She is always learning something new to introduce into her life (energy, business creativity, human design, spiritual related)! She loves sunsets, time spent in nature, singing karaoke, dancing at every music event she attends, spending time with her friends, and boyfriend in her downtime.

Jennifer's personal journey of triumph over financial struggles, emotionally abusive relationships, self-abandonment, and sugar addictive behavior has led to the creation of two businesses aimed at helping individuals shed the "Weight of Armor." In addition to being a published author, she now expands her outreach through public speaking events, guest speaking on podcasts, future books and blogs, collaborations with fellow entrepreneurs, somatic movement classes, community resources, group coaching, and personalized one-on-one coaching—all with the shared goal of fostering healing and growth within her community.

For more information on how to work with Jenn, connect with her on FB (@*FAB Approach*) & IG (*@fabapproach*), for the announcement of her community resource group, coaching programs, speaking events & even an upcoming book reveal in 2024!

the word that cannot be spoken

Lisa Heath

W hen you are backed against a wall with no way out what do you do? When you get the worst news over and over what do you do? We all have these moments in life. Some of us more than others. How would I flocking know? Like, who am I? Lisa Marie Heath!! LOL

I've discounted my own ability for so long. Always shrugging nonchalantly and saying, *"That's just what I had to do, it's life."* I wake up and do what needs to be done. Right there is exactly what my issue was. I didn't take the credit for the hard work that is my day-to-day existence. I have had the first thought of my day be, *"I'm better off dead, no one would miss me and then I wouldn't have to deal with all the pain and trauma that is my life."* And every day, I choose to recenter myself and get up every morning and face life once again. So, before I go into how I can do this every day, you need to know a timeline of events to put all of this into perspective.

- Adopted 2 days after I was born, followed by my (adopted) parents telling me at the age of 8.

- 2000-2009: Years of pain and my body betraying me to finally be diagnosed with Mesothelioma Ovarian Cancer at age 21. Yes, the one you see commercials for on TV. *If you have been exposed for extended periods of time to asbestos. Please call.* Crazy to find out, I was 1 of 4 people in the world to be diagnosed with Mesothelioma in an area of your body that was not the lungs. Treatment at that time was removal of the ovary before it spread. Every 3 months I had a follow up with my oncologist and reproductive doctor. During those months I did 2 rounds of IVF to save my eggs if I decided later down the road, I truly wanted kids.

- 2008: My Best friend and Fiancé passed away from a motorcycle accident. 3 months prior to when we were to be married.

- 2010: Graduated from Florida State College of Jacksonville with my Associates of Art Degree with a focus in psychology.

- 2012: I fulfilled the requirements to graduate with my Bachelor of Science degree in Psychology and a minor in cognitive behavioral with an honors Thesis (on identity and adoption) from the University of Central Florida (go Knights).

- October 2017: Thrown from the back of a golf cart that caused my brain to bleed. As well as breaking 3 ribs and 3 vertebrae, 3 facial fractures, and 3 fractured bones in my neck. I would find out later, that the blow to my head caused the bleed resulting in me having a Traumatic Brain Injury (TBI).

- December 2017: Graduated with my Masters in Ministerial Leadership and Church planting (Leader and business side of the church) from Southeastern University.

- 2018: Found out my ovarian cancer was back. This time, treatment required a total hysterectomy, catapulting me into menopause at 34. Oh, and still dealing with TBI recovery. 6 months of hell trying to figure out the right cocktail of medication that keeps my body stable.

- 2019: Hospitalized with Chemical Pneumonia, the cause being how a vape battery heated up the liquid in a vape in August of that year. I was in a coma and on a ventilator, the doctors telling my parents one of the worst things a parent can hear, *"Prepare for the worst. We have done everything we can do. She is dying more every day."* Needless to say, I beat the odds and warn everyone I can about the effects of what could happen if you vape and was featured on my local news stations because I beat the odds.

- 2020: Finally able to focus on retraining my brain, but with restraints of a gag order not to talk about or do much because of a lawsuit having to do with the crash. It was rough to navigate. I'm used to standing out and they wanted me to be plain Jane. Thank you, Lord, for all the help to restrain me. I wasn't even allowed to ride the brand-new John Deer Tractor, that rode better than my car. My tractor has lights and turn signals, and I was able to drive it at night. LOL. Joke's on them.

- 2022: I took a gamble and attended a personal development training. It was a HUGE investment, and leap of faith really. I knew then what my purpose was back on earth. Why did I choose that event? Because I was meant to. I have had many mentors and been told the same thing about network marketing. It only got me so far in business before I would start to doubt myself. A downward spiral would be what came from my doubts, belief in myself and being the failure that I've always been told. This man spoke to me on a psychological level that helped me figure out the deeper connection to my true purpose. Now, I have the support of a community of like-minded people who help each other grow in our impossible crazy dreams.

That brings us to today. Overcoming obstacles on a day-to-day basis is how my life goes. Full time caregiver/advocate for my amazing parents and myself, a daughter of God, author, founder of HEATH foundation & advocate for those who suffer in silent because it is taboo to talk about suicide. Overcoming whatever is thrown my way with love, laughter & a silver lining every day. God has given me purpose through being that advocate for my parents and I can say with 100% certainty that the reason I am alive today is because of my parents, my dog, and faith. Without any of those, I would have given in to those suicidal thoughts back in early 2018. So, I truly know what it means to be in that deep abyss and not see a light at the end of the tunnel. But I am also living proof that there is a light.

The brain is capable of just about anything, the battle for my life was just beginning when I woke up from the crash in 2017.

My first thoughts when I woke up in the hospital and a lot of days since is, "*Why am I even here?*" I wake up for my parents, the people who are watching, and the people who need help but don't know how to ask. Flock, it's still hard. Prior to the crash, thoughts of ending my life never crossed my mind. Now it is one of my default settings that I consistently battle. But every day I say to myself, "*I will do the best I can for that day.*" Some days all I can do is make it out of bed. I am not going to lie. I have begged God to take me out. I have recorded videos of me crying mouthing I just want to die, but I never do. I still have those problems, but far less now than I did in the beginning. It has taken 6 years to rebuild my life to the closest version of myself that I used to be.

I have felt alone in trying to process these thoughts. When I would talk to family and friends about how I was thinking about killing myself, they would say, "*Don't say things like that. Don't talk like that, get that out of your head.*" I didn't have a safe place to speak. No one wanted to even listen to what was going on with my thoughts. I guess they thought that the pain and depression was why. No one realized I wasn't okay.

Even with my own doctors, or therapist. Their first response was, maybe we need to discuss admitting you to be watched. I always had to back pedal quick to reword it. Doctors would commit me if I told them about all my thoughts of wishing I was better off dead.

The subject and the word "suicide" is taboo. Everyone tends to go on high alert rather than focusing on the feeling of hopelessness and feeling adrift. I have a background in psychology, and I wasn't prepared enough but the tools I learned and the faith I have, have helped more than I ever imagined. Thank you, to the higher powers, God, and my angels for honestly preparing me for this situation.

I had to put those tools and faith to work by being my own advocate. Without injuries, the world is hard, stressful, and chaotic for some of us. Try multiplying that by 10 to 20 times and you will be in the scrambled mess I call my brain; trying to navigate life with a brain injury created more problems with becoming overwhelmed and stressed with day-to-day activities. I wanted to off myself. My body stayed in fight or flight mode, truly never knowing what was going to happen. The thoughts of not feeling worthy, not being an active member of society, a waste of space living with my parents. I felt defeated every day, while I was bitching about something the whole flocking time. I hated the world and shared that. I was the victim, in the nightmare I was living in. I never gave in; I did give up. While my education tremendously helped. It wasn't enough.

NOTHING WAS!!!

And I mean nothing...for instance, alcohol didn't help. I started to become an avid drinker after my crash, because drinking was the norm for the guy who was taking care of me and his friends. They were all alcoholics, and I quickly followed in their paths. You are the product of who you hang with. The drinks in the end caused my condition to worsen. Not to mention, if I kept drinking my brain would eventually shut down and I may not wake up.

Part of the consequences of the TBI was starting to have black outs, or even "red outs" which are fueled by rage. There were many mornings that I would wake up after a day or night of drinking and notice bruises on my body. My boyfriend at the time would never tell me much of what happened, just saying, *"Lisa, that was yesterday. Today is a new day."* If he had marks on him, I would harp on him to tell me what happened, but he only told me about my episodes that were over-the-top batshit crazy.

Here are the top 3 episodes:

- 2 months after injury, December 2017: I was convinced that the 2 guys I was living with were out to get me. Both men were the cause of my crash and so I had every right to think that, at least if it happened. Again, I am going by what they told me. Apparently, I locked myself in the dog cage a few separate times. When I was in this state, I called former friends, who had been out of my life for years at this point, to help me or to come get me. I had no idea who I called until the next morning. They had no clue what was going on. One of my church friends drove across town to pick me up and take me to my parent's house. The next morning, when I woke up, I was totally confused about what had happened.

- Jan 2018: After New Year's, my boyfriend picked and picked at me until I blew up. I locked myself in the bathroom to get away from him, at least that was my thought process, I think. LOL. Turns out he kicked, or body slammed into the door just because I wouldn't open it. But I was the one who was told to leave the house. I am thankful my parents let me come back home, especially given the way I had been acting since the crash.

- 5 months after the crash, March 2018: I was arrested for domestic abuse. The irony, I was the one that called the police. While driving home after happy hour with my boyfriend and his friends, we got into a huge fight that I have no recollection of. All I knew was that when my brain woke up and processed it was in trouble, it was already too late. I was in the back of a cop car, in handcuffs with my mom yelling at me to not say a flipping word. Then she asked if she could take my glasses. Still having no idea, I looked out the front of the cop car window, to see my boyfriend laughing with the police officers. Oh, I was enraged. He was the asshole who always caused the fighting. And I was the one being arrested, WTH?!? Once at the county jail that's when I finally found out what I was being arrested for...Scratches!! Flocking Scratches! Were they kidding. That was all!!!! He didn't get punched or beat to hell. No, he had scratches so that's all they cared about, since they spoke and saw his marks before mine. The call that was made to the police department was a domestic abuse call. It was a flocked-up adventure that was unnecessary. However, if I had not called 911 because he wanted to drive, I would have never been in that situation. He had a record of a DUI. I'm assuming I called to give them the plate numbers. Worst night ever. It was not a fun experience. It lasted 11 hours and I will never go back.

This is what my life had come to. I was a shell, walking around wishing my brain would shut down, and that I would just pass away in my sleep each night. Things continued getting worse and worse by the day, physically, mentally, and emotionally.

While my lawyers did their thing behind the scenes, I continued looking for a full-time job because it seemed like the right thing to be doing at the time, even though this wasn't even a full year after the crash, and only a few months after my arrest. The positions I was applying for were career jobs with relatively SIMPLE skills and tasks that are used over and over. My therapist and I figured it was worth a shot. Why not? Neither of us knew if it would be a good fit or not.

After 3 long months of applications and interviews, I was hired at Bank City working with cardholders on one of their many Visa card programs. Woo Hoo! Lisa finally landed a big girl job. But let's go back to the timeline...2 weeks before I graduated from my training and started taking live calls...my cancer came back. A total hysterectomy was my only option. Followed by pelvic floor therapy. At the beginning of the new year, I was able to start back with Bank City and this time around I was prepared to jump through hoops for special accommodations that my body needed to perform the job they had hired me to do.

Once we finally knew what was going on, life revolved around my therapy. I was able to FINALLY start therapy to retrain my brain, my memory, and my hand-eye coordination. 3-4 times a week at the neurologist's office. 1-2 appointments a week to my clinical therapist.... And this went on and on EVERY WEEK FOR 2 YEARS. This was my routine. If you were to look in my planner from those years, that is all you saw. And oh yeah, the rest of my life with parent responsibilities and my day job when I could attend work. That planner was, and still is, my life. If I scheduled something I always had to have my calendar. I learned the hard way if I agreed to something without my planner I used to double or triple schedule shit. Writing everything down is still necessary. I forget from one room to the other. My brain was a fog of emotions that took over.

For example, Without the medication in me. I will cry off and on all day over everything. I thought my laughing was a defense mechanism. Nope, it is just my brain doing what it wants to do. I thought I was the one in control. Man was I wrong.

How do I know the medication helps and keeps my brain working "right?" Because medication changes after my hysterectomy. Remember how I said we had to try and figure out how to regulate my body? Well, one of the new PAs in the neuro office suggested we work on switching my medicine because according to them, *"The ones I was currently taking were no longer working."* However, 4 weeks later I am screaming at this PA for everything that has happened since changing my medication. Screaming for the whole office to hear how unstable I was, flying off the handle, and not able to get a grip on my reality. Her exact words were, *"If you are that unstable, committing you may be the best option. For us to help you."*

Well, if you thought the office could hear me before, they really heard me telling her, *"You want to take me away from the only things keeping me stable, my parents and my dog. You have lost your mind."* By this point the head doctor was walking into the room. They never changed that main medication again. That was why for the first 3 years no one knew about the voices in my head.

Don't let it be said that Lisa Heath isn't a risk taker. I was willing to be the guinea pig for my neurologist, who specialized in trauma, to test all new experiences and treatments. If they had a new tool to help with my condition, I tried it. I wanted to be as close as possible to who I was prior to the crash. I was determined. If I was going to stay on this earth, I needed all the skills that were offered. If they said it could help, we did it. Even with all the push back from my brain.

But it wasn't just medication and brain re-training that worked. It was determination, faith, trust in those I loved, and finding purpose in day-to-day activities. Also, sleep...recouping the energy spent in battling this constant pain.

To whoever is reading this, you are the first ones to know my true thoughts. This is the first time I have spoken so openly about those dark thoughts. No one knew until now how my brain works. I am now here for all of you who have thoughts that no one will listen to. I had to do it on my own. I didn't have a choice but to survive. It is my desire to forge a pathway of understanding so that no one else has to do it alone. I am working on bridging the gap between the taboo of suicidal thoughts, suicidal ideations, living will mental illness, and striving for mental health. I am looking to break the cycle of silencing those in the greatest need and shining a light on the similarities we have, rather than the differences. Most of us are flocked up even if we don't look or act like it. Some of us are just really good at faking it. I want us to be real with ourselves and those we love.

So here is one last thing I want to share with you all. It is a motto I created to say when life gets hard and out of my control. It has become a thing I say at least once a day now.

"I'm alive and delighted. Thank you, Jesus, for another day. I stand here before the Lord and the universe; my commitment is strong My faith is my focus Watch out world you're not ready for my SPARKLE. Allow my shine to show others that it can be done. From this moment forward, I know believing in myself is the first step, staying grounded and never ever, ever, ever, forget how far you have come. Bless the future for I am capable, determined and a fiercely fabulous woman."

So, it is my wish for you all dear readers to show the world your SPARKLE, to believe in yourselves, and remember that you are capable, determined, and fiercely fabulous.

Love each of y'all, XOXO & God Bless

about the author
Lisa Heath

Lisa Marie Heath is a professional researcher and student with a love of psychology, along with her interest of how neurological cognitive behaviors effect the brain. After spending 10 years in college, she is an achieved master in business and leadership. Lisa had a come to Jesus moment that catapulted her life into the direction of becoming an author, motivational speaker, advocate for her parents, and herself. Her passion is to help others with brain injuries and their caregivers, by providing resources that were unavailable to her during her own healing journey. She is in the process of starting her foundation, The "Heath Foundation," which means,

*H*elping
*E*veryone
*A*ffected by
*T*raumatic brain injuries
*H*eal

When Lisa isn't in her superhuman form, LOL. You can find

her assisting with something her father is getting into at home or in their garden. SMH. :) She's a God-fearing woman who can always be found where any dogs are. Her love of dogs keeps her busy when she isn't at home with hers, she can be found taking care of other family's fur babies. Lisa loves to travel and if she isn't at home or fur-baby-sitting, she's simply gone on another exciting adventure. Wheels up and ready to go!!!

For more info about how to work with Lisa visit her website (www.lifeoflisaheath.com), connect with her via FB, IG, or send her an email (lifeoflisaheath@gmail.com).

there is no finish line
Ally Robinson

Imagine the color green. No, not the color of a crisp Granny Smith Apple or a lit-up Christmas tree. No, not the color of a sparkling emerald or a lucky four-leaf clover. Imagine the color of guacamole that's been sitting out for far too long. Vomit. An ugly bridesmaid's dress.

In my nightmares, this horrible green surrounds me. It consumes me. Green paints the walls. Green in the cheap carpet on the floors. Green, green, green covers the long hallway in my dreams...

I wish it were just a dream... but a nightmare goes away once you open your eyes. The details of your dream slip away throughout the day.

But no matter how much I blinked, pinched my arm, or bit my lip, I still lived this nightmare. No, not a dream... my reality.

I was forced to walk down this green hallway. Although my walk was more of a hobble as I supported my weight on the walker before me. My arms shaking as I struggled to hold myself up.

Why the hell am I still here?

How the heck did I end up in this condition?

Just days ago, I was a sophomore in high school, dancing and twirling on my toes, preparing to perform in the ballet rendition of Sleeping Beauty. And now it's taking all my willpower to get my grippy-sock-cover feet to move across this hideous green flooring.

But then I remembered... the pills...

Pill after pill, after pill...

I swallowed the pills one by one... becoming more sure of my decision with every swallow.

On the night of March 26th, 2011, I took a prescription medication concoction and laid down on my bed, perfectly content that I was ending my life, and I would never wake up again.

Which is why I was so damn confused to be walking down this hallway.

I am dead... right?

Is the path to hell really a green hallway? I guess I'd imagined more fire and pitchforks. I mean, I couldn't possibly be going to heaven. Even at 15, I had experimented with too many drugs, had way too much promiscuous sex, and told too many lies to have a chance at entering the pearly gates.

I tasted blood and noticed a hint of pain from where I was biting my lip.

I became hyper-aware of my throbbing headache, the burning sensation in my stomach, and the ache of every muscle in my body.

Can you feel pain in the afterlife?

A realization sucker-punched me in gut...

I was alive!!

My heart was still beating...

What the actual fuck.

I wanted to cry.

I wanted to scream.

I wanted to just lay down and DIE...

Instead, I had two nurses guiding me down the hallway to my room in the behavioral health unit.

The reality that I was going to have to live hurt.

If I couldn't even be successful in killing myself, how the hell was I going to be successful in life?

Walking down this horrible green hallway was my first test.

Every step was agonizing; the pain in my head was excruciating, yet I gritted my teeth and kept walking...

IF... I could make it down this hallway... maybe... just maybe, I could endure life.

I made it down that hallway, spent a week attending therapy, eating jello, and playing team-building games with other troubled teenagers held hostage in the behavioral health unit. They let me go home at the week's end, claiming I was rehabilitated.

While I never made another attempt on my life, I was far from cured of my self-loathing and suicidal ideation.

I never attempted to take my life again, primarily out of fear of failing rather than fear of dying. I lived life in this autopilot daze.

I had no dreams, no desires, no goals, no passions.

I did what everyone told me to do, or what I thought I was supposed to do when I "grew up."

I actually met my husband several years later, when I was 19. Very shortly after dating, I got pregnant, had a baby, and we got married.

Yet I still wasn't happy.

Don't get me wrong, I love my husband, and being a mom is the best. But even when I had the "perfect life," I still lacked the spark and desire to live.

I was still going through the motions... hoping my depression and anxiety would stay suppressed enough for me to hang on.

Ultimately, I realized that I needed to make some serious changes.

I couldn't keep living in fear that one day, I would take my life and leave my little boy without a mom. I wouldn't be able to grow old with my husband.

I needed something to live for outside of the endless laundry, a job I hated, and the thankless tasks that come with motherhood.

I needed something to drive me forward.

I needed something to be passionate about.

I needed a goal.

One day, while mindlessly scrolling, I came across an ad for the Miami Marathon.

A marathon, hmm...

I'd always wanted to run a marathon. Watching my dad run and receive medals was one of my most vivid childhood memories. I mean, my dad got an actual medal just for getting up and going for a run. I wanted a medal. Thus, running a marathon has been on my bucket list for as long as I could remember.

Now, while I've always been somewhat athletic (thank you, years of ballet), I was definitely NOT a runner. Outside of those memories of watching my dad run marathons, I knew nothing about running. But I needed a goal. I desperately needed something to live for. I needed something for myself. I needed a medal.

There are no awards for most loads of laundry washed in a day. No gold star for cooking your family a nutritious meal every night. No pats on the back for waking up with a crying baby every night... Nope...

But I could get a medal for running a marathon. I could get a medal and recognition for being part of the 1% of the world that runs 26.2 miles.

So, I started training… Not very well.

I made mistakes, did too much too soon, and got many injuries, but I pushed through.

And, I wasn't on autopilot anymore, I was taking control of my life.

I began looking forward to each day. I started enjoying motherhood a whole lot more now that I had my own dreams and goals. I got promoted at work. My life was transforming with every mile of training.

On the morning of my race, I was terrified. My husband held my hand as he drove me to the start line.

"You got this, babe." He said as I got out of the car.

I stood there at the start line among thousands of other runners. Listening to the National Anthem Ring out. My eyes teared up. As if I knew… that my entire life was about to change. This was the turning point in my life… And I was NEVER going to be able to turn back.

The cannon fired, the race started, and I ran… well, by Mile 7, it was much more of a limp. My lack of thorough training was showing. My IT Band flared up and was angry. Like really angry. It screamed at me with every step I took. But I kept going.

My husband met me at Mile 22. I cried into his arms…

"This is NOT FUN"

"Why did I do this to myself?"

He dried my tears and laughed as he told me that he would see me at the finish line.

Every step after that was excruciatingly painful. I dragged my feet on the asphalt. I started seeing GREEN.

That same awful putrid green that haunted my nightmares.

I was back in that hallway.

Fear washed over me. I needed to sit...

Miles 23...

MILE FUCKING 23.

I had come so far but still felt so far away from finishing 26.2 miles. So, I sat down, and I cried... consumed by my green hallway. I could quit. I could stop. Right here, right now. But I know what it's like to quit. I already tried to quit on life... and it landed me in a zombie haze...

No joy, no passion.

No, I couldn't live like that anymore. I couldn't quit. I cried harder. This time, not because of the pain. But because I knew I WAS GOING TO HAVE TO CONTINUE. I stood up. I gritted my teeth and walked down my hallway... When I opened my eyes. my gripped socks had been replaced with running shoes snug on my feet, and my hospital gown was now sweat-stained running clothes. My hallway was the streets of Miami, and my final destination was the finish line...

If I could make it down that hallway, I could FUCKING finish this race.

So, I ran.

I crossed that finish line. My husband was there cheering me on, and I felt something I had never felt before.

PRIDE.

For once in my life, I felt PROUD of myself.

I did this! I didn't give up.

I didn't quit.

I ran a marathon.

I knew at that point I could never quit again. That I was capable of ANYTHING I put my mind to. My entire life really did change.

That was my first of many races. I educated myself about how to train properly, avoid injuries, and prepare myself mentally and physically for the excitement, exhaustion, and celebration that came with each race. Every day I could feel myself getting faster, stronger, and able to run further.

With that first race, that first medal, I proved to myself that I was capable of accomplishing big things. Scary things. And it became my life's mission to help other women achieve their goals.

To help them conquer and overcome their own green hallways. To see themselves as strong, powerful, capable, worthwhile, and enough.

No matter how many races I run, how many medals I win, and how many finish lines I cross, I now understand with absolute certainty that life isn't a race, and there really is no finish line. At least not if we're doing it right.

whatever it takes

about the author
Ally Robinson

Ally Robinson is a professionally trained ballerina and model, turned certified personal trainer and running coach. After discovering running as a way to save herself, Ally set out to share what she'd learned with others and has been helping unstoppable women reach their goals since 2019 through strength training, mindset work, nutrition, and of course running. Ally works with her clients 1:1, as well as within her small group weight loss mastermind challenges, and offers a variety of self-paced courses to help even the busiest of boss ladies with revamping their relationships with food, exercise, and their own self-confidence. Ally has also created a variety of journals for runners of all levels, tackling everything from nutrition and weight loss to mindset and race training,

available for purchase on Amazon. For more information about Ally, her courses, journals, and upcoming races, visit her website at www.somethingrunderful.com, follow her on social media (@something_runderful), YouTube, or check out her podcast **Something Runderful** on Spotify and all other major streaming platforms.

whatever it takes

the first rule of entrepreneurship

Mandy Schulis

W hen Megs and I decided on naming this book "Whatever It Takes", I didn't know how many feelings and thoughts this would bring up. I have started and stopped this chapter more times than I can count because telling you the truth about what it's taken for me to be successful and what that means to me is a bit like Fight Club. And the first rule of Fight Club is "You don't talk about fight club". If you don't get the movie reference, Google it. Brad Pitt is HOT. Real talk, though. The first rule really IS not to talk about it because the behind-the-scenes shots are the one no one wants to know about, right? Wrong. I'm pretty sure you want to know and that's exactly why you picked up this book. The premise behind the entire movie, not to be a spoiler, is that that main character is in a fight with himself. Who he fantasizes about being versus who he really is. The funny part? They are BOTH him. Brad Pitt's character Tyler doesn't really exist, it's all in his psyche. I feel like that's an accurate representation of my journey and what creating a business feels like, a fight between yourself and the Universe, that continues until you are in the position in space and time that you are supposed to be. Your "purpose" of being here on this earth. The real spoiler is, there are WAY more rules to doing whatever it takes. And because I'm breaking my "code of silence" about my journey, I'm going to give you all the ones I've discovered, or at least the most important ones. I'll even tell you how I've broken them because, after all, rules are made to be broken, right? Hold on to your hats and your tatas, it's gonna be a bumpy, wild ride.

The first rule about entrepreneurship isn't one that you can control or even use, really. It's more of a truth than a rule and that truth is "you don't choose entrepreneurship, it chooses you". While you might've chosen or are choosing to start a business, I guarantee there's a reason that pushed you to do so. It might be necessity. For me, I've been a caretaker and a mom for 13 years. I couldn't hold down a nine-to-five if my life depended on it. Not because I don't work hard, quite the contrary, but because I take care of a high need's child and both of my parents. My daughter's illness is tricky. She'll be ok for a few months and then... well, definitely not. It's a genetic shitstorm of immune suppression and collagen deficiency which means she is sick and injured more than she is "normal". Whatever normal means anyway. I swear, the cruelest tricks life plays lie in unseen illnesses. I am lucky that so many of my clients understand and have dealt with similar situations. The fierce love I have for my family and my dedication to my daughter's condition are two major reasons I will never make it somewhere with an HR department.

Ella is obviously a full-time job by herself, but in addition to that, I took care of my dad for ten years after his stroke and my ex-husband for several years as well, as he lost his fight with addiction. Both are passed on now, but, because the Universe has a sense of humor, I also have a 2-year-old "Wreck It Ralph", Ella's brother Beau. And he's, well, TWO. If you're a mom reading this, I can hear you laughing. You get the picture. I have simply accepted that caretaker is one of the innate roles the Universe has assigned me.

The second rule of entrepreneurship is "always expect the unexpected". I mean that from both a great truth and a horrible underestimation of crisis potential. You've heard of Murphy's Law, right? That has never been truer than with creating and running a business. What do I mean? I mean literally everything can change in an instant. For me, I created my first company I met a former NFL player's wife, thinking nothing more than if she liked me, she's possibly book with me again. The next day, I was summoned to the front desk to answer a phone call. Thinking it was my then fiancé, I answered, babbling on cheerfully. After a distinctly long pause, a deep voice responded, "I don't think I am who you think I am". I was stunned, stammering my apology. After he questioned if I had worked on his wife the previous day, I was nervous, thinking surely, I was in trouble. Then, he asked if I had time available that afternoon. I didn't, truly. But I made time, even though I knew how tired I would be adding a two-hour massage session to an already overloaded book. It was the smarted decision of my life.

That one decision led to me forming my own company a short 6 months later, traveling and being on call for over a dozen starting professional athletes, all paying $200/session, often twice a week. There's a country song that talks about 1 year you're getting your truck repossessed, the next you're buying a jet. Entrepreneurs know that this is not only possible, but plausible and probable. It all comes down to the moment everything changes. The only real bitch is that you never really know when that moment will be, you just have to stay ready and prepare the best of your ability.

While I love happy endings, I'll also share with you two of the toughest situations I had to finagle out of and how I managed to come out singed, but still standing. Both are finance related, and I'll take this time to point out that if you start a business or are a current owner, take the time to find out what your credit score is. Not your personal score, although that is important, too. Your business credit score. While your personal is super important, none of that matters with business loans or lines of credit. Just trust me and you can thank me later, but that isn't the point I am making here. I'm not in credit or anything to do with money. I'm an energy and bodyworker turned mindset biz coach. I don't ever want to tell people what to do with their money. However, especially as a woman, I am a HUGE advocate of knowing what your options are and how to use them.

The first tough situation was when I left my abusive marriage for the second time. Yes, you read that right. I divorced him twice. I really like to dig into my bad decisions and make sure that they are truly terrible ideas. That's not part of this book, though I promise I'll tell you the full story about that in another one. Because of the first divorce, I knew there was no way in hell I was going back for round 3. I was rebuilding my massage practice after being part time to care for Ella and certainly wasn't making enough to maintain a household on my own, especially with a custody battle and paying for Ella's medical alone, which was how I wanted it, but DAMN those numbers were scary.

I did the only thing I knew to do. I leveraged my credit. I charged it and or I bartered for it. I found people that had what I needed and found a way to pay them, either through massage sessions, herbal remedies, whatever I could use short of happy endings or getting on a pole. I got very good at knowing which cards I could pull cash advances from and what the limits on each were. I made sure I applied to extra credit cards, so I had them to use when the divorce hit my credit and my score tanked. Within a year, most of them were maxed out, but I'd created a six-figure business again, and was making headway each month little by little.

Then Covid hit and the world froze. In 2020, I was given a reprieve from the massive payments and could breathe for the first time in 2.5 years. I started hearing about economic impact loans and disaster recovery grants. I ignored them at first because, thanks to the kindness of my landlord and my clients, I was able to pay my rent on my shop. Then, I got to thinking. Everyone else plays the finance game, I really should see what my options are, even if it's a dead end. That turned out to be one of the smartest things I ever did. Applying for a Small Business grant and loan allowed me to pay off some of the credit card debt and my lawyer. It also bought me some time to not work as hard when we found out that, SURPRISE, we were pregnant with Beau, who was high risk and still to this day, I am convinced tried to kill me.

Having good business credit and a long-standing history literally saved my business, but it also allowed me to make one of the hardest decisions ever required of me, shutting it all down. We'll talk about this more in a second, but the Universe had been sending me signs for a couple of years, from constantly being ill, to an unplanned high-risk pregnancy and finally, nerve damage in my hands that prevented me from holding my newborn, much less continuing my massage practice. Right about here is when I got PISSED. I mean, for frick's sake, when was enough ENOUGH?

That leads me to the third rule of entrepreneurship, "your business will never end up being what you think it will be". You'll start out as one thing or performing one service and SOMETHING will happen to change all that. I like to tell my client that the Universe nudges, then it shoves, then it bitch-slaps you. And the way it does that is most applicable through the entrepreneurial journey. After all, you're trying to change the world and fulfill your life's purpose, right? Well, sister, I am here to tell you, be careful what you wish for.

I may sound snarky when I speak about bitch-slapping and not knowing what's next, but if I'm honest. There are always clues. I knew that my time as a massage therapist was done. I was just too scared and worn out to admit it. I knew I was meant for more, that I was meant to do greater things and help people on a larger scale. But the thought of starting all over terrified me. I mean, just writing those few previous paragraphs touching on what the previous ten-ish years was like made me tired. Can you imagine what it was like living it? But, if I'm honest, I had spent the better part of my life preparing for what was next, which is how I ended up coaching female entrepreneurs on their amazing stories.

And up at bat, we have rule number four, "pay attention to the skills that are transferable, no matter what business you're in". I mentioned I was angry when I retired from my massage practice. The truth is that I was grade-A boiling over MAD, so it took me a bit to realize that, while I could no longer use my hands to heal or relieve pain, I had already been "coaching" for many years without knowing it. On top of that, I had been giving away much of my business knowledge for free for longer than I care to think about. I remember telling my husband Matt that if I could teach other female business owners my mindset... my thought process... I'd be a millionaire. His response was "So, why don't you?" Gotta love men, right? They are so literal and simple. And in this case, right. As I launched my "what's next" plan after subleasing the shop and refunding my massage clients, I started doing digital marketing and social media, but it just didn't feel right. It felt similarly to when I tried to be a recruiter in the corporate world post college, kind of like a jacket I could get on but felt like I should be Tommy Boy singing "Fat Man in a Little Coat". That's another cult classic you should watch if you haven't.

Then came the day that the truth hit me like a lightning bolt. So much of my massage practice was based on personal stories and trauma, from the NFL player that was injured and scared to get back out on the field, to the woman leaving her marriage and starting over, to the billionaire business mogul who suffered from neck and throat issues because, honestly, his father was a bastard and he felt that in order to be successful he had to model his behavior. We did a TON of facial release and throat chakra work. SO MUCH of their pain was mental, but more importantly, it was in their STORY and the stories they told themselves. Thus, Mandy the "Story Coach" was born.

My final and fifth rule for entrepreneurship is "trust the process and lean into the unknown". Or more simply, "what is yours will always find a way." You might've picked up that I am a bit woo-woo from this chapter, but I am serious. If it's not meant for you, nothing in the world can make it happen for you, but if it IS meant for you, nothing in the world can stop it. And you'll know it in your gut. I did, when I knew my massage career was over, just like I did the first time I got on stage and talked about using your personal story to un-fuck your mindset. Yes, that really happened, and it IS recorded. There's also a bit about using your story strategy to create an identifiable brand because, after all, even us woo-woo people are strategy driven.

Trust me, I look back on the last almost two years and I have zero idea how I got here in terms of the steps from A to B. I was even discussing with a dear friend today about how I always came up with the money to invest in the things I needed to move forward. I always met the right people at the right time. I always heard EXACTLY what I needed to hear. I feel like the Universe has been nudging me along this latest path and if I'm honest, my gut is now telling me that this is the one I was being groomed for all these years. The business experience and the hardships have all been to prepare for this moment, so that I can teach and inspire other female entrepreneurs to just GO FOR IT, as I truly hope you will.

To recap, here are my 5 Rules for Entrepreneurship:

1. You don't choose entrepreneurship, it chooses you.

2. Expect the unexpected.

3. Your business will never be what you think it will be.

4. Pay attention to the skills that are transferrable.

5. Trust the process.

I'll leave you with this. Maybe now, you see why entrepreneurship is like exactly like Fight Club. Most don't talk about it because it IS scary and if we told the truth, who in their right mind would sign up for literally fighting with yourself to build a legacy... to become the version of ourselves that both thrills and terrifies us? Only crazy people, right? But, let me tell you something, in the words of the great author Lewis Carroll, *"we are all a bit mad here."* You must be a little bent to sign up for this. You're in a good company. We are the ones that dream bigger, love harder and aren't satisfied with the status quo. We are the ones that want to change the world and are crazy enough to think we can. Hold on to those five simple rules and I promise, you'll shock even your biggest critic, which more than likely is... YOU. Keep the faith and keep going. Your purpose is waiting.

about the author
Mandy Schulis

Mandy Schulis is a serial entrepreneur with 2 successful businesses under her belt, an MBA in Entrepreneurship and Marketing, plus a digital marketing certification. She's a certified, trauma-informed story coach that helps female entrepreneurs bust through mindset barriers and teaches them to leverage their stories for income and impact. Mandy believes in authentic conversation and connection above all else.

After launching her 3rd business in 2021, she pivoted from marketing services to coaching, after realizing that many successful female entrepreneurs get stuck in their own stories, often resulting in Imposter Syndrome and fear of success. Whether these women are going through divorce, recovering post-partum, launching a brand-new business-it is Mandy's ability to help them see where they fit into their story that is her superpower. This process had been coined Mandy's

signature method, The Story Shift. Her belief is that every story has a purpose and yours is the key to creating a life full of purpose, profit and fun. She is a domestic abuse survivor, former single mom and believer in fairytales. She currently resides in Tampa, FL with her husband Matt, kids Ella (12) and Beau (2) and her 2 rescue fur babies that are always at her feet when she's writing!

You can find her at www.mandyschulis.com or under Mandy Schulis on Facebook and Instagram.

just write
Megs Thompson

S ometimes doing whatever it takes means setting and upholding a boundary to protect our own energy and well-being. Sometimes it means saying no when everyone else thinks you should be saying yes. Sometimes it means shutting off your cell phone, unplugging the Wi-Fi, and sitting in absolute silence, holding long periods of meaningful eye contact with your dog in a desperate attempt to feel seen, heard & understood.

Sometimes doing whatever it takes means hiding in your office and fast forwarding to 'that' moment in *Return to Me* where Minnie Driver & the gorilla connect - because you know it'll be exactly what you need in order to release the pressure, break down, and set loose the flow of snot bubble filled tears you've been fighting to keep hidden for far too long.

Sometimes doing whatever it takes means admitting to yourself and others that you're human. *I know - shocker, right?*

Add to the equation being not just a woman, a wife, a friend, a sister, a daughter, and an aunt, but a successful business owner, and sometimes doing whatever it takes means prioritizing a particularly white-glove client over a family dinner, camping trip, or weekend of catching up on your own creative writing projects.

It's nearly impossible to accurately explain biz ownership to someone who hasn't done it. In fairness, it may also be because they still have their senses while most entrepreneurs I know have lost more than a handful of their marbles along the way and would do it all again in a heartbeat. It's almost like trying to tell a teen today about life back before Spotify, Google, and AI. *Trust me kids - it was a completely different world.*

Believe it or not, when I first joined the rat race known as corporate America some 20+ years ago, I was extremely shy, insecure, and absolutely terrified of being called out for being uncool. This may come as a surprise to those who know me today. What can I say, it wasn't until well into my 30s that I finally stopped wasting my energy on worrying about what others might think of me and started living my life on my own terms. I tossed that bucket of fucks out the window and stopped waiting for someone else to turn on the light at the end of the tunnel. I lit that bitch myself.

But, before this happened, before I started prioritizing myself, my dreams, my desires, and my plans, there were years where I spent nearly every waking moment doing whatever it took, to appease, connect with, and please others. Sadly, because of how shy and awkward I felt in most social situations, doing whatever it took meant partaking of far too many substances to inhibit my quirks, dull my hesitations, and amplify what little excitement I could muster for the crowds of people I was meant to be networking with.

Before I knew it, I found myself relying entirely on my new friends Molly, Mary Jane, Jose, and Hendricks just to fit in, to connect with others, to smile, to laugh, to make conversation, and to feel comfortable. There are years where it's easier for me to tell you the times I was sober, than the times I wasn't. These behaviors, these friendships, that had started as a means of easing my discomfort, became a necessary part of my daily life.

While I could feel at the time that what I was doing was wrong, that I was masking my true self in order to show up as who I was expected to be, I was surrounded by a world that reminded me numerous times daily about what 'normal' looked like. What 'normal' sounded like. How 'normal' acted. Solidifying again and again that at my core, in my natural shy, insecure, quirky, offbeat, snarky state, I was not, nor would I ever be, considered normal. And, in corporate America, the name of the game is fitting in. Being normal. Fitting the mold and following the well-beaten (*boring af*) path ahead of you. No questions asked. *Seriously. Don't ask questions.*

Then, something happened. Well, in truth, a lot of somethings happened. First, I met a pretty amazing guy. A man who had dealt with his own demons and addictions, but who introduced me to the idea that being me, naturally me, was more than enough. He loved me more than I ever thought possible and reminds me that he still does each and every day. Then, on a random Tuesday, after working 60+ hours in only 4 days, I woke up and realized that I hated my life. Absolutely hated it. I was spending my days doing whatever it took to make money for a faceless corporation that didn't care how ragged I ran myself, so long as their bottom line was met. I was managing a team and doing my absolute best to shield them from the expectations being set by the powers that be but knew in my heart that I really wasn't a very good actress, and my team knew me well enough to see through my feeble attempts at telling them, *everything's fine.* Then, a good friend of mine passed away in an accident. She was young, gorgeous, hilarious, brilliant, and in a moment, she was gone. She'd had her entire life ahead of her, and the biggest plans of what she was going to do with every moment. She was doing whatever it took to bring her big crazy dreams to life, but then, just like that, those opportunities were gone.

That's when I finally realized that I was spending my life doing whatever it took to please others. To make them feel comfortable, confident, accomplished, and fulfilled. All the while wasting my life and my paychecks on countless substances just to numb the hatred I had for my own existence. Too often, as women and business owners, we get caught up in our innate desire to be a caregiver. To nurture and empower others, to the detriment of ourselves. Our well-being. Our hopes, dreams, passions, and purpose. We see prioritizing ourselves as being selfish when in fact, by doing whatever it takes to pursue our own happiness and fulfillment we're setting an example for others that it's okay to want more, to be more, to be, dare I say it, genuinely fucking happy!

So, I gave myself an ultimatum of sorts. I had one year, to either figure out a way to love the life I was living (ugh) or to live a life I loved. Writing and telling stories has been my favorite pastime since I was a child, in fact, I have a journal from when I was about 7 years old, where I wrote that when I grew up, I wanted to listen to old people talk about their lives and turn them into books. But, somewhere along the way, I'd gotten so tied up in the stress of fitting in, being 'normal,' and making a living, that I'd lost sight of that passion and become just another faceless cog in the machine. I set about figuring out a way that I could still pay my bills, but also feel excited about my life. I no longer wanted to rely on forces and substances outside of myself just to exist.

I spent nearly every waking moment of the next few months figuring out how to build a website, register a business, form an llc, and pry myself from the claws of the corporate monster. The first iteration of my business, *megswrites llc*, was focused on providing professional copywriting services to small business owners, something I was very good at (*if I do say so myself*), and while it still didn't quite light me up in the way I craved, it was unbelievably better than what I was spending my days doing during my full-time job. I continued signing clients, providing them with client-attracting copy for their websites, sales pages, ebooks, blogs, online articles, and social media posts, all the while knowing that I wanted more.

Only a few days shy of that 1-year goal, I officially gave notice at my day job and became a full-time professional copywriter. Already I was happier than I'd been in years, and I knew that there was no stopping what I'd started. Over the next few months, I was approached with 2 ghostwriting opportunities, and immediately, I knew that this was what I'd been waiting for. I shifted the focus of my business from copywriting to ghostwriting, and in the last year, I've added editor, cover designer, and publisher to my resume. Now, I spend every day doing what I love most, playing with words, my own and those of my clients. Taking our stories and experiences and turning them into books that fill shelves around the globe.

It's funny, looking back, how selfless I thought I was being, by putting myself last, prioritizing everyone and everything else above myself, when in fact, it's now, when I'm doing whatever it takes to achieve my own big crazy dreams, prioritizing my own happiness and fulfillment, that I have people reaching out to me daily, sharing how much they appreciate my authenticity, my quirks, my snark, and my voice.

about the author
Megs Thompson

Megs is a professional work-twerker, book-doula, intuitive writing coach, ghostwriter, author & publisher based in the heart of Montana. After spending 20+ years trying to fit into someone else's box in the corporate world, afraid of what might happen if she swam against the current, Megs decided to leave her health insurance, paid vacation & regular paychecks behind to start her own business, following her passion & purpose only a few months before the world caught on fire (2020). Now, 4 years later, Megs has not 1 but 3 businesses, all booming (yay!), has moved from the Pacific Northwest to the Frigid Rocky Mountains (brr!), married the love of her life (aww!), adopted not 1 but 2 puppies (wtf was she thinking?!), published 15+ books of her own & 50+ for her clients (more in the works), and is loving life more than EVER!

When she's not playing with words, Megs can be found exploring rabbit holes & fueling her slight obsession with all

things true crime, coffee, cryptids, and cults, or working on her latest quilting project.

For more info about how to work with Megs and get your own story on the shelf, visit her websites, www.megswrites.com & www.inomniaparatuspublishing.com, connect with her via FB (@megsthompson), IG (@megs.writes), or send her an email (megs@megswrites.com). You can also join *just write: accountability & educational community for writers* for inspiration and motivation for your own creative writing projects.

the 3 stages of choice

Amy Woods

The words she was hearing were new to her. They were things she'd never been told before. She'd been conditioned throughout her entire life to believe that choice was not a part of her circumstances. That she was guilty by assumption. That she was guilty by association. That her choices were made merely out of spite. That her choices had to be for the wants of others.

It didn't matter that she was a child, mourning her family after a bitter divorce that she'd been thrown into the middle of. Mourning the passing of her father and being told how much of a better-behaved child she would be once her dad had died. Her choices were gone for what seemed like a lifetime.

So that day, as she woke up in a hospital bed, she was confused as to why the one choice she'd made, the one choice that no one else should have had a say in, didn't happen. She was mad. Raging mad. Being told that she had a choice meant nothing to her. They were just words that slithered past her ears as she blocked out the notion of ever trying to do something on her own, without the input and pressure from others. At that moment, she chose to not choose.

Sitting there, thinking back to the time her life fell apart, she saw it. She saw the accusations, the mistrust, the uncomfortable fact that strangers and outsiders trusted her more than the people closest to her. No matter how much she pled to hear the truth, her cries fell on deaf ears. She saw that she manifested their mistrust to come true, she made their disbelief happen, and she chose it because the truth was never believed. Only accusations were believed. Assumptions. And if others around her were doing "it" she was incapable of not doing it herself.

Without realizing it, she was making choice after choice, never understanding why she made the decisions she did. Why she felt she had to prove everyone right. Why she felt that she had to believe what they believed. Why, since the age of 12 she'd gone along with what everyone else said was right so willingly, without question. She continued to choose what had been chosen for her until she knew she could choose differently.

I'm Amy Woods, Founder of Women Choosing Excellence where I educate women on the power of choice and how choice comes in the power of 3.

The night I woke up in the hospital was the aftermath of trying to take my own life. I never do anything small, and when I was tired of living with the pain of what I felt I had no choice in changing no matter how hard I tried, I drank almost a half-gallon of whiskey, and placed a loaded pistol in my mouth, ready to fire. I woke up in the hospital 4 days later.

To say I was disappointed is an understatement. I heard all the pleas of getting sober, going to work, and going after the SOB that took my kids away from me. I heard and felt in the actions of others that I wasn't worth anything. I could see the shame in their eyes and had a squad of victim cheerleaders in my corner, telling me, "It's going to be okay," and "You're so strong."

I was exhausted from having to be so strong my whole life with no choice in it. I was angry, pissed off, and taking my life was the only thing I felt I had a say in. Drinking to blindness and seizures was what I had control over.

I don't know what made me decide that that was my only choice at the time, but I was choosing to stop the pain, stop the noise, and stop the grief of wanting life to be good, easy, and peaceful.

I chose, but life chose me instead.

The next day when the nurse came back on shift, she sat in the chair beside my bed, and she asked me what brought me to that point.

She was easy to talk to and came in without judgment wanting to know my story. Not to tell me what to do next. It was refreshing.

I told her about the divorce, that I wound up homeless, and how that led to me losing my kids. How my ex, the person who used to love me, was okay with allowing me to be homeless. He was okay with allowing my kids to see their mother in that state. How he then sued me, taking away my kids, while I was living in my car. I chose to send them back to their father when this happened because I chose my children's well-being. I refused to allow them to be homeless. I didn't want that for them. I wanted their life to remain as normal as possible. I also knew the outcome of what was going to happen the day they left my house. I knew they would be lost forever after that. It's what that family does.

Grieving my children while they were still alive. Being told that I was just the woman who gave birth to them. That I was the lowest person in the world to them after all that I'd endured to try and keep their family together; broke me. Mentally, I had a mental break is what they called it. I couldn't handle the stress and on top of it all, I had no one. No family. No friends. No support.

As I told this story to the nurse, she asked me, *"So what now? What are you going to do now? You can't go back to doing what you have been doing."*

I ask her, *"What can I do? I have no money, no car, no family, no job. I was just dating someone who I truly loved but he was in the same self-destructive phase himself due to his own loss and grief."*

She asked if he was good to me, and I told her, *"Yes, he's as good as he can be at this time. He is the best person I have ever met."*

She asked, *"What do you want from here?"*

I replied, *"I have no options."*

She stated, *"You always have a choice. That is what is amazing. From this place, right here right now, you have a choice to create life in a way that is what you want, without anyone else telling you how you should live, without anyone telling you what you have to do, without anyone telling you what you want is wrong. You have an enormous amount of opportunity right here right now at your fingertips."*

She was right. In the moments of utter despair, the biggest opportunity of my life showed up. The opportunity to create a life that only I chose to create, where I chose who could be a part of it and choose how fast I'd allow it all to happen.

This pivot point was the first of my 3 choices.

The fact is life happens in 3's and choice follows this same concept.

I chose to leave my ex. I chose to give my kids back. I chose to try and take my life.

Going back even further. I chose to marry my ex. I chose to have kids at a young age. I chose to allow him and his family to control and mentally abuse me.

Wait you chose that? Yes... Part of allowing new opportunities to flow in is taking responsibility for the choices we make, made, and are making.

I have been an active participant in my life for the past 46 years. Of course, I didn't see that at the time all of this was happening. That isn't how our brains work. It takes choosing to allow forgiveness. Choosing to allow happiness and reflection along the way to understand where our responsibility lands in our lives.

It takes understanding that you do what you know until you know to do better.

That day in the hospital bed at the deepest of disparities was the best moment of my life. It's the day I chose me.

For the first time in my life, I chose me. I could. I was allowed to. I was the only one who could deny that choice and the only one who could give myself permission to choose me.

I was truly, at that moment, the most independent I had ever been in my life. I was no longer a victim. I was no longer being made to survive. I was no longer just making it and going along with it. All in a wisp of a moment. A fleeting second. I didn't see it while I was sitting there, but the thought that I could choose something changed everything.

I got to work that night, barely sleeping, thinking about what it was I wanted in life. No one had ever asked me what I wanted to do with my life, what I was passionate about, or where I wanted to be in a year, or 5 years' time.

I had never had time to even consider this for myself. I felt lost, scared, and free.

That night I decided I wanted a degree. I wanted to excel at something. I had left school in the 9th grade and earned my GED. I wanted to prove to myself that I was good at something. So, as I was sitting in bed I enrolled in college. I chose creative writing for my major because it had always been a dream of mine to be an author. I wanted to be known in ways that no one ever believed I'd be capable of accomplishing. I was a creative person, had a lot of stories in my mind begging to be written, and wanted to be like Danielle Steel.

I enrolled in college not having any money, not knowing how I would pay for it, not knowing how it would all work out, if my boyfriend and I would actually make it through this, or if homelessness was going to be my future. I had no idea where I was headed, I just knew it was up. Forward. Moving away from the life I had lived for the past 40 years. I chose me. Choice number 1... Choosing yourself. It's the hardest choice you will ever make.

There will never be approval for it, and often, you'll find yourself not being supported. You are, after all, changing the "HOW" in how people see you. It's different and in the act of choosing yourself, you are placing boundaries of what was; what was normal, and what was familiar, and changing that.

That choice is lonely, isolated, and uncomfortable. Who was I after all, if I wasn't taking care of everyone else first? Who was I, if no one was telling me who I should be? I felt the most independent in my life at this time, and at the same time, I was the most vulnerable, lost, and lonely.

The next step in my story of choice came when I chose to heal. On our journey of choosing excellence, we often feel the power of survival, of resilience. But this isn't healing. Healing comes when you are challenging your mind's beliefs, values about yourself, and the habits that you have created along the way, that your mind perceives as normal. This is also true about how you see yourself. It's a habit. It's a value that you take action on.

If you feel the need to always settle for less than what you truly desire, this is a value you act on with the mindset that you are not worthy. You are not deserving. Or you are not enough. The actions are often letting go of our desires, our wants, and our self-care, settling for half of it or nothing at all.

This will show up if there is emotional business left over to deal with.

I had a recurring dream that was based on a release meditation that I often did. I would be in a room in a basement with a lot of doors. Behind the door I always chose was me trying to escape and get to whatever it was I wanted. However, the room was filled with a worm-like creature that reminded me of tar. Every time I took a step forward it would encompass me and hold me back, keeping me in the room. What was really interesting was that it felt safe. Familiar. At home.

In this dream, my desires were on the other side of that door. My success, my happiness. The dark past was holding me in my comfort. The comfort of what I was used to. This is how I knew, based on my intuition, that I had to heal in order to transform my life into what I wanted.

In my personal life it was showing up in ways that I couldn't see until my husband pointed out that he wouldn't stay in our marriage the way it was going. It kind of stopped me in my tracks because my husband isn't the kind of person to want out of a relationship... He knows that marriage has its ups and downs, and he isn't one to argue.

I was raging though. I was so angry about my past, the life I was dealt, my sorrow was eating at my soul. I would think he wanted other women just from him looking in other people's direction and that would set me off on a 3-day self-destructive bender of rage, crying, anger, shaking, not getting out of bed, and ready to flee the scene. I now realize this was my fight or flight pattern and reaction that I was doing. Waiting for the other shoe to drop. Why be comfortable when everyone in my life had always left me.

There was never anything permanent and I never really ever felt at home anywhere. Lost in a sea of just existing.

My degree, which switched from creative writing to communications with a marketing focus and professional writing minor, wasn't going to suddenly create a life of healthy choices, happiness, and joy, and move me away from a life of circumstances I wanted to change.

I had to heal, look at myself differently, and understand how this played into every part of my life. In my relationships, in my business, in my love life, in my own personal relationship with myself, with my kids, and so much more.

So, this time I chose to hire a coach who was big on mindset work, and that I knew could hard-hand me where I needed her to at that time. Again, I had no idea how I would pay for it. But I was choosing to heal so I could create the circumstances I wanted in my life. I hit submit on my investment, and it left $50 in my bank account.

At this time, I hadn't remarried yet, and my now husband had no obligation to help me in this investment because it wasn't his burden. I personally believed that because he hadn't caused the situations I was facing, why should he be responsible for helping pay to fix them? I didn't communicate with him that I had just spent $5,000, and I didn't have to. The mere fact that I chose me, and chose to heal, opened up the space for money to support it, to come in. I had called out to the universe what I was doing that was uncomfortable and fully believing that it was the HOW to make my desires come true and I was rewarded for it.

When you choose and make choices that are different from what hasn't worked over and over again in the past, you open yourself up to opportunities in ways that you don't expect, and for everything to just work out. This is why you don't have to know the how, you just have to act.

My money came in the way of a refund for overpaying child support from the state. Guess how much? It was $4,000. It took care of what I had just invested.

Now the real work was able to begin on my healing journey.

By choosing to heal, I let go of what other's perceptions were of me, of the control, of the bad habits picked up along the way, of the feeling of unworthiness, lack, and being undeserving of love, relationships, and money. I built a self-confidence I've never had. My past self-confidence was based solely on how I could attract people with my body. Now I walk into a room with a presence that is indescribably magnetic and attractive. This has been a 3-year journey, but my life is different. I changed the circumstances I was born into and that I had continued to create in my life.

The third step in this choice process is probably the most powerful, the most scary, and the most rewarding.

After healing, I knew I wanted to help other women to do the same. But I isolated myself in a way to keep myself safe, behind a computer in my own home, in my own space. Until the opportunity came when I was able to meet these people, in person, these individuals with whom I had shared my journey.

Again, a large investment, but I jumped in. $7,000, and again not knowing how I would pay for it. How is this a major step in choice? This is where I chose to move forward in my life. To step away from safety. To step away from my past. To step away from hiding. To step away from being codependent. To step away from who I have known as Amy and into who I was becoming.

It was the most powerful choice I've ever made. You hear stories of kids escaping captivity and this felt similar to that.

I met women who showed me a mirror, supported me to make bold moves, and create a commercial for my business. Women who I connected with at a soul level and when it was over, I cried like a baby, releasing who I was when I first stepped into that room. Into that hotel. Into the presence of those amazing humans.

I chose to move forward and leap into my desires. No action plan. Not knowing how. Without the need to have it all figured out and for the first time in my life I trusted. I trusted myself. I knew it was what I had to choose. I knew that I was who I had to choose.

By choosing to move forward, I learned things about my past in my childhood that I didn't remember even happened. I allowed myself to pull my energy away from my past and move it into my present life. I learned that if you are giving all your energy to your past, you cannot have any left to be fully present in the life that I was living now and creating for my future. I learned I cannot love myself fully as I deserved if I was too busy hating my past self because I am one in the same person. I learned I couldn't fully give love to others if I had none to give to myself. Keeping my heart locked in the past.

To open myself up I had to do a lot of releasing, meditating, and breath work. I had to learn to allow my feelings fully and how to release them. I had to understand I could do this work and choose to be happy and proud of the work I was doing.

My entire life has opened up to new and amazing opportunities since that weekend. I have been speaking, writing books, selling my offers, and getting closer to my husband in ways I couldn't have imaged before. I am doing things I love to do, helping women in ways I have always dreamt about, I am traveling more, and doing more in my community. I chose!

The power of choice transforms your life into the life you want to live, one small boulder at a time. Every choice you make moves that small boulder until you reach the top of that mountain. It's ALL POSSIBLE.

My journey has magic to it. It's a journey of possibilities. I will forever be grateful for my journey and for that day in the hospital... It's what's allowed me to make the 3 choices I needed to, in order to create a life of joy, fulfillment, and happiness.

The choice of self, the choice of healing, and the choice of moving forward. The 3 stages of choice to create a life you love.

whatever it takes

about the author
Amy Woods

Amy Woods is a sales empowerment coach, a women's empowerment advocate, and a speaker for online and in person events. With a BA in Communications as well as 7 advanced leadership certifications specializing in personality studies, Amy thrives most when she's coaching her clients on everything from how to create authentic connections, to the power of networking for a business's sales. Amy is especially passionate about the belief that there is always a choice to create new circumstances in life and that we are not the product of our past but the product of what we are currently creating in our lives.

Through teaching women to empower their soul traits, and who they are at their core, to embody what they desire, and to use what they are talented at with passion, Amy has helped women heal from past trauma, rediscover themselves

 after a major life event, and discover how to apply their journey to their business. When Amy speaks at local and national events, she creates a path for women to release their past and move forward. She also helps corporate leaders adopt a standard of excellence while reigniting their own passion for

their career to better encourage the excitement of their teams, resulting in more productive weeks and months, increased revenue, and a more cohesive company culture. These services have been perfected through Amy's businesses and services; Infinity Sales Systems, Escorting Yourself to Excellence, Women Choosing Excellence, and A.R. Woods Consulting Network, LLC.

Amy has overcome homelessness, alcohol abuse, losing her children through divorce, suicide attempts, and years of mental and emotional abuse. She graduated from college, has built a successful business, and remarried the love of her life. This is how she knows without a doubt that nothing is never impossible. Amy's mission is to ensure that all women, regardless of where they come from, see how powerful their choice is, and how powerful they truly are on the inside. She also is on a mission to bring back company cultures that are structured around the concept of family orientation, real connections, and embracing each other instead of competing. This allows companies to thrive and create a happy working environment where some of the women Amy works with have a chance for the success they desire.

You can connect with Amy by visiting her website www.womenchoosingexcellence.com, follow her on social media (FB @amywoodsbusinesscoaching, IG @amywoodscoaching, LinkedIn @amywoodscoaching) or by sending her an email (amywoods@infiitybusinessdevelopment.com). Amy's podcast, *Shut Up and Dance* is available on Spotify, YouTube and most other major streaming platforms.

epilogue
Mandy Schulis

S torytelling isn't just a fun concept, it's a way of life. It's in our DNA as humans. It is a powerful skill that transcends every barrier possible, from centuries to cultures. It is a way to teach, preserved and explain the things in life that aren't always easily explainable. Storytelling is a way to create an authentic connection, literally. When people share their stories with one another, there is a concept that happens called a "mind meld", where neural coupling happens. An emotional story can trigger a release of Oxytocin, i.e., the "love hormone" which creates bonding, trust, empathy, and compassion. This is a nerd's way of saying we literally absorb one another's stories.

In these pages, you have read the stories of women that have truly done whatever it took to go after the life and dreams they desired. These aren't just stories; they are an example of what can happen when you choose to not obey the rules. To choose to tune out what others say is possible or impossible.

This book started in the hearts of two little girls that always knew they were different and turned into a mission to share the stories of other "little girls" that grew up to be women dancing to their own beat. We hope that you have bonded and felt the power behind each of these stories because they are messages of hope and resilience-true examples of doing whatever it takes to fulfill their dreams. If you are wondering if your story matters, it does. There is someone out there that needs to hear your story, to learn your wisdom and to know that they can succeed no matter what.

mandy

m² storytellers inc